Apartheid by Stealth

An African Whistleblower

Table of Contents

PREFACE: Apartheid by stealth. An African whistleblower.

"This is no time for wearing the shallow mask of manners. When I see a spade, I call it a spade." Wilde.

Then, crooked, and insatiably greedy bastards won in compromised courts, but in the war, when the corporal flipped, the only true Judge looked away, and they lost everything - John 5:22.

Scotland, England: Kevin Atkinson (NHS Postgraduate Tutor, Oxford) unrelentingly lied under oath—Habakkuk 1:4.

A Racist Crooked Brainless Scotchman.

New Herod, Matthew 2:16: Closeted hereditary white supremacist bastards must control all Africans, and Africans they cannot control must be 'legally' destroyed.

Racist descendants of thieves and owners of stolen human beings hate us, and we know - Habakkuk.

New Ya'akov: Like Jacob, who deceived his own blind father for material gain, they are professional deceivers, impostors, and experts of deception.

BEDFORD, ENGLAND: District Judge Paul Robert Ayers, > 70, a Mason, and the Senior Vice President of the Association of Her Majesty's District Judges, of 3, St

Paul's Square, MK 40 1SQ, how many charitable works did charitable Masons do before SLAVERY? Ignorant descendants of THIEVES and owners of stolen poor black children of defenceless Africans, including the African ancestors of Meghan Markle's white children—Habakkuk.

Integrity, Friendship, Respect, and Charity.

Conflict of interest; Then, under their law, the PROTECTORS of Africans against racial hatred were closeted white supremacist Mason Judges, and their overriding objective was the continuing propagation of their institutionally racist legal system – Habakkuk 1:4

"This and no other is the spring from which a tyrant springs, when he first appears, he is a protector." Plato

.

BEDFORD, ENGLAND: GDC, Mason, Brother, Richard William Hill (NHS Postgraduate Tutor) fabricated reports and unrelentingly lied under oath - Habakkuk 1:4
A Racist Crooked Freemason.

Before familial racial hatred unravel, they are always conspiracy theories, but when hereditary racial hatred and uneducated racial intolerance unravel, they instantly mutate to innocent mistakes.

"Ignorance, madam, pure ignorance." Dr Samuel Johnson

Our opportunist racist white bastard District Judge wants to help African children by destroying their father.

A white wolf in white sheep's clothing.

Putin used guns to steal Crimea. European Christians used guns to dispossess Native Americans, and they stole their land. The white Catholic Irish ancestors of President Joe Biden did not evolve in America - Habakkuk.

"All have taken what had other owners, and all have had recourse to arms rather than quit the prey onto which they were fastened." Dr Samuel Johnson.

"Affluence is not a birth right." David Cameron (a former premier).

"Freedom of Expression is the cornerstone of our democracy." The Right Honourable Jacob Rees-Mogg (MP).

'Judiciary in England and Wales 'institutionally racist', says https://www.theguardian.com › law › oct › judiciary-i…18 Oct 2022 — Exclusive: more than half of legal professionals in survey said they saw a judge acting in a racially biased way.'

Based on very, very, proximate observations and direct experiences, all functional semi-illiterate white Freemason Judges are RACIALISTS.

"Someone must be trusted. Let it be the Judges." Lord Denning (1899 – 1999).

All white Freemason Judges are human beings. Some human beings are RACISTS.

"All sections of UK society are institutionally racist." Sir Bernard Hogan-Howe (a former Metropolitan Police Chief).

Freemasonry Fraternity and Judiciary are parts of UK society.

"Although white people with points of difference suffer prejudice, they have not suffered the same racism as black people. It is true that many types of white people with points of difference, such as redheads, can experience this prejudice. But they are not all their lives subject to racism. In pre-civil rights America, Irish people, Jewish people, and Travellers were not required to sit at the back of the bus. In apartheid South Africa, these groups were allowed to vote. And at the height of slavery, there were no white-seeming people manacled on the slave ships." The Right Honourable Diane Abbott, Cambridge University Educated Historian, Lawyer, and MP.

Based on cogent, irrefutable, and available evidence, nearly all Nigerians in Great Britain, irrespective of tribe or tongue, and including some Ekweremadus, are victims of HEREDITARY RACIAL INTOLERANCE.

Meghan Markle is a Nigerian, albeit 43% genetic Nigerian.

43% is a very, very, significant pass mark, even at Oxford.

"The first class at Oxford, where I have examined, is an overrated mark." Hugh Trevor-Roper, 1914 – 2003.

Our Genetic Nigerian (43%): "Meghan Markle was the victim of explicit and obnoxious racial hatred." John Bercow (a former speaker).

"Racism is rife throughout most organisations across Britain." Sadiq Khan, the Mayor of London.

"White supremacy is real, and it needs to be shattered." Dr Cornel West.

The Guardian's news about racist white Judges is not new news to self-educated Nigerians in Great Britain.

There is no new news under the sun. The only thing new is that closeted white supremacist bastards are no longer very, very, good at concealing INNATE RACIAL HATRED.

An opportunist hereditary racist white bastard was granted the platform to display hereditary prejudice.

Quasi-Communism: Then, when white Solicitors and Barristers failed in practice (predominantly but not exclusively white), and loads did, if they were Freemasons, they became Judges or something else, and if not, they became Politicians or something else.

1976–2022): Having FAILED in practice, lots and lots of white lawyers did (predominantly but not exclusively white), instead of becoming a politician and doing the Estelle Morris, he joined the Freemasonry Fraternity (Mediocre

Mafia, New Pharisees, New Good Samaritans, Defenders of faiths, including the motley assembly of exotic faiths and religions associated with the 15 Holy Books in the House of Commons, and Dissenters of the Faith – John 14:6), secured a very, very, cushy salaried job where he had daily dialogues with white imbeciles (predominantly but not exclusively white adults with the basic skills of a child), and he securely parked his liability very, very, close to the public till, and for three-fourths of his professional life (more than three decades), and he exchanged crass mediocrity and confusion for very, very, valuable consideration: A perfect white supremacists' scam.

Their grossly overrated, overhyped, overpopulated, and mediocre trade is dying slowly and imperceptibly: Too many lawyers, not enough work.

"The legal system lies at the heart of any society, protecting rights, imposing duties, and establishing a framework for the conduct of almost every social, political, and economic activity. Some argue that the law is in its death throes while others postulate a contrary prognosis that discerns numerous signs of law's enduring strength. Which is it?" Professor Raymond Wacks.

Based on available evidence, English Law is equal for all blacks and all whites, but its administration isn't – Habakkuk 1:4. The administration of English Law is a myth.

One day, Negroes will protest, but not riot about Apartheid by stealth, and to balance the unbalanced, the nomination, and constructive appointment of Judges by Lords will be based on transparent, colour-blind, and measurable objectivity, then, and there will be merit based diversity that will, at last, reflect the entire multi-ethnic and multi-cultural Britain, and the administration of English Law will no longer be tyrants' tool – Habakkuk 1:4.

Based on cogent, irrefutable, and available evidence, right now, homogeneity in the administration of English Law is the impregnable secure mask of merciless racist evil – Habakkuk 1:4. Racist evil – ne plus ultra.

JUDICIAL DIVERSITY: ACCELERATING CHANGE. "The near absence of women and Black, Asian and minority ethnic judges in the senior judiciary, is no longer tolerable. It undermines the democratic legitimacy of our legal system; it demonstrates a denial of fair and equal opportunities to members of underrepresented groups, and the diversity deficit weakens the quality of justice." Sir Geoffrey Bindman, KC, and Karon Monaghan, KC.

"The white man is the devil." Elijah Mohammed (1897 – 1975).

Based on very, very, proximate observations, direct experiences, cogent, and irrefutable evidence, the white man isn't only a devil, he is also a THIEF.

NORTHAMPTON, ENGLAND: Based on available evidence, GDC-WITNESS, Dr Geraint Evans, Postgraduate Tutor, Oxford, unrelentingly lied under oath (on record) - Habakkuk 1:4; John 8:44; John 10:10.

A RACIST WHITE WELSH CROOK.
'He is a typical Welshman, usually violent and always dull." Wilde paraphrased.

Their skin colour is universally acknowledged to be irrefutably superior, and their intellects aren't, and their legal system is fundamentally designed to conceal that truth.

They brainlessly and baselessly self-awarded the supreme knowledge, and they think it is their birth right to be superior to all Africans, and when they realised that Africans are not inferiorly created by Almighty God, they criminally stole yields of our Christ granted talents, and they impeded our ascent from the bottomless crater into which their very, very, greedy, and sadistic racist bastard ancestors threw ours, in the African bush, unprovoked, during several continuous centuries of the greediest economic cannibalism and the evilest racist terrorism the world will ever know – Habakkuk.

Then, very, very, highly civilised, transparently ultra-righteous, super enlightened white European Christians were greedier than the grave, and like death, the insatiably greedy racist white bastards were never satisfied – Habakkuk 2:5.

ACHROMATOPSIA: Greedy racist white bastards could see blacks in the dark, but they cannot see their own white kindred in bright light.

Transparently just equitable reparation pends, and several continuous centuries of unpaid interest accrue.

Then, theirs was a bastardised, indiscreetly dishonest, unashamedly mediocre, vindictive, potently weaponised, and institutionally white supremacist legal system that was overseen by Members of the very, very, Charitable Freemasonry Quasi-Religion (Mediocre Mafia, New Pharisees, New Good Samaritans, Defenders of Faiths, including all Faiths and/or Religions associated with the 15 Holy Books in the House of Commons, and Dissenters of the Faith—John 14:6)—Habakkuk 1:4.

"To deny or belittle this good is, in this dangerous century when the resources and pretensions of power continue to enlarge, a desperate error of intellectual abstraction. More than this, it is a self-fulfilling error, which encourages us to give up the struggle against bad laws and class bound procedures and to disarm ourselves before power. It is to throw away a whole inheritance of struggle about the law and within the forms of law, whose continuity can never be fractured without bringing men and women into immediate danger."—E. P Thompson.

INTRODUCTION: Dr Ngozi Ekweremadu

"Of black men, the numbers are too great who are now repining under English cruelty." Dr Samuel Johnson (1709 – 1784).

They have unbounded and unaccountable power, so they criminally use it to steal superiority, which they brainlessly and baselessly associate with the universally acknowledged irrefutably superior skin colour that they neither made nor chose, and which they somehow believe is their birth right.

The only truth is that they hate us, and we know, and they will tolerate subservient Africans. Ignorant descendants of THIEVES and owners of stolen children of defenceless poor people awarded themselves supreme knowledge, and they used incompetent racist lies to conceal hereditary intellectual impotence, and they guarded the centuries-old unspoken myth that the universally acknowledged irrefutably superior skin colour that the very, very, fortunate wearer neither made nor chose is related to intellect.

Based on available evidence, white supremacist Mason Judges are the most potent, most powerful, and most dangerous enemies of African Negroes—in Great Britain.

BEDFORD, ENGLAND: GDC, Sue Gregory (OBE) lied.

A CROOKED RACIST OBE OF OUR EMPIRE OF STOLEN AFFLUENCE—HABAKKUK

Proxy War: A Negro (Nigerian) versus Freemasonry Fraternity.

All proxy wars desire imbecilic pawns.

Our white protectors are not colour-blind: Judiciary protects Social Order.

"This, and no other, is the root from which a tyrant springs, when he first appears he is a protector." Plato.

Conflict of interest: Then, the most important part of the job description of closeted hereditary white supremacist Mason Judges was the preservation and continuing propagation of the indiscreetly institutionally racist legal system that paid their wages, and concomitantly, they were tasked to protect the interest of the principal officers of their indiscreetly institutionally racist system – Habakkuk 1:4.

Then, if an Officer of the Most Excellent Order of our Empire was a racist criminal, it was the responsibility of closeted hereditary white supremacist Mason Judges to bury racial hatred, selflessly, but criminally, in pursuant of the preservation and the continuing propagation of their indiscreetly institutionally racist legal system that paid their wages, hence the conflict of interest – Habakkuk 1:4.

"Jews are intelligent and creative, Chinese are intelligent but not creative, Indians are servile, and Africans are morons." Professor James Watson (DNA) paraphrased.

Then, when Nigerians made serious allegations of racial hatred against white people, white people who oversaw the administration of their law will investigate the serious allegations made by Nigerians, and when they find that they were based on truths, they will pass them to Genius Jews, their GO-TO-PEOPLE, and they will try to legally justify racist crimes, and if they couldn't, they will try to criminally bury racial hatred, and if they couldn't, they will try to bury the witness and/or victim of racist crime, and how, all loose ends must be tied by all means necessary.

They are professional racist criminals, and if you can see them, and they know that you can see them, you have inadvertently reached the end of your life, as the loose end must be tied by hook or by crook.

Ignorant racist white bastards (predominantly but not exclusively white) weren't deterred by His Justice (John 5:22, Matthew 25: 31 -46)—because decorticate shallow racist white bastards (disproportionately but not exclusively white)—did not believe in His exceptionalism (John 14:6).

White Privilege: Then, the powerful and very potent leverage of closeted hereditary white supremacist bastards was their whiteness. The invaluable whiteness that they neither made nor chose.

White Privilege: Sometimes, one wishes one were white, so that one could experience and enjoy the sweetness and privileges of whiteness.

"Out of the blackest part of my soul, across the zebra stripping of my mind, surges this desire to be suddenly white. I wish to be acknowledged not as black but as white …... By loving me, she proves that I am worthy of white love. I am loved like a white man. I am a white man. Her love takes me unto the noble road that leads to the total realisation …...I marry white culture, white beauty, white whiteness. When my restless hands caress those white breasts, they grasp white civilisation and dignity and make them mine." Frantz Fanon (1925 – 1961).

Based on available evidence, Comrade Pol Pot was born in 1925, Dr Frantz Fanon was born in 1925, Patrice Lumumba was born in 1925, Anthony Benn was born in 1925, Mrs Thatcher was born in 1925; they are all in Jannah or inside Dante's Inferno.

"The most potent weapon in the hands of the oppressor is the mind of the oppressed." Steve Biko (1946 – 1977).

Then, the most potent weapon of closeted hereditary white supremacist bastards, the direct descendants of the father of lies (John 8:44)—was the mother of RACIST LIES, and their power was the absolute certainty that Judges will be white, and their hope was that the Judges will be closeted hereditary white supremacist bastards too—Habakkuk 1:4.

Psalm 144: Then, hereditary racist bastards lied that they didn't lie, and they lied and lied, and lied again, to their mentally gentler children that they were very highly civilised ultra-righteous Christians who were guided by the sword of transparent truth and did everything legally: The rule of law.

"The sword of truth." Jonathan Aitken

Then, incompetent racist lies were told by incompetently mendacious racist white bastards (predominantly but not exclusively white), and before their incompetent racist lies unravel, they were conspiracy theories, and when they did, they instantly mutated to innocent mistakes.

"Lies are told all the time." Sir Michael Havers (1923 – 1992).

BEDFORD, ENGLAND: Based on available evidence, District Judge Paul Robert Ayers, > 70, a Mason, and the Senior Vice President of the Association of Her Majesty's District Judges, unrelentingly lied under oath (on record), or otherwise verifiably deviated from the truth on record— Habakkuk 1:4.

Facts are sacred.

"The truth allows no choice." Dr Samuel Johnson

Bedford's District Judge Paul Robert Ayers, > 70, a Mason, and the Senior Vice President of the Association of Her Majesty's District Judges, 3, St Paul's Square, MK 40 1SQ: White man, let me tell you, the mind that the Nigerian got is finer than the indiscreetly institutionally racist legal system you serve, and it is possible to use cogent facts and irrefutable evidence to irreversibly destroy you and it.

The fellow told the truth, in the Council, before Jews and Romans —when He disclosed pictures His unbounded mind painted - Matthew 27:1-2, 11-26.

OXFORD, ENGLAND: Helen Falcon (MBE), Member of the Most Excellent Order of our Empire, a former Member of the GDC Committee, a former Postgraduate Dean, Oxford, a very, very, charitable Rotarian (charitable Freemason), and the spouse of Mr Falcon - unrelentingly lied under oath (on record)—Habakkuk 1:4.

OYINBO OLE: A Racist Crooked Member of the Most Excellent Order of our Empire of Stolen Affluence— Habakkuk.

Facts are sacred, and they cannot be overstated.

WHITE PRIVILEGE: Had the white woman been black or had the Judges been black, the crooked closeted hereditary white supremacist bastard, Member of the Most Excellent Order of our Empire of Stolen Affluence - would have been in trouble.

Former Judge, Constance Briscoe, attempted to spin Police Officers, she was punished.

Then, all Judges were white, and they were ultra-righteous, and they did not tell lies and they did not steal.

"Lies are told all the time." Sir Michael Havers (1923–1992).

OUR OWN NIGERIA: SHELL'S DOCILE CASH COW SINCE 1956.

A brainless racist white bastard whose white mother and father have never seen crude oil - is our District Judge in BEDFORD.

What's left when racist Judges use incompetent racist lies to conceal hereditary racial hatred – Habakkuk 1:4?

OYINBO OLE: Unlike Putin's Russia, there are no oil wells or gas fields in Bedfordshire and where his white mother and father were born.

Our own money, Nigeria (oil/gas), is by far more relevant to the economic survival of his white spouse, his white father, his white mother, and all his white children than NORTHAMPTON. The white ancestors of his white mother and father were THIEVES and owners of stolen children of defenceless Africans, including the African ancestors of Prince Harry's white children – Habakkuk. Helen Falcon, a racist crooked Member of the Most Excellent Order of our Empire of Stolen Affluence and Sue Gregory, a racist crooked Officer of the Most Excellent Order of our Empire of Stolen Affluence, are principal officers of the state, and in pursuant of the preservation and continuing propagation of their indiscreetly crooked and institutionally racist legal system, closeted hereditary white supremacist Mason Judges, selfishly, and criminally buried the RACIAL HATRED of their own white kindred, as their own pockets desired it.

It is absolutely impossible for all white Freemason Judges in Bedfordshire (predominantly but not exclusively white) to use cogent facts and irrefutable evidence to disprove the truth that Bedford's District Judge Paul Robert Ayers, > 70, a Mason, and the Senior Vice President of the

Association of Her Majesty's District Judges, of 3, St Paul's Square, MK40 1SQ, unrelentingly deviated from the truth under oath (on record)—Habakkuk 1:4.

If all the white Freemason Judges in Great Britain (disproportionately but not exclusively white) could disprove the truth that Sue Gregory (OBE), a racist crooked Officer of the Most Excellent Order of our Empire of Stolen Affluence—Habakkuk, unrelentingly lied under oath (on record), and if they could disprove the truth that Helen Falcon (MBE), a racist crooked Member of the Most Excellent Order of our Empire of Stolen Affluence—Habakkuk, and if they could disprove the truth that Bedford's District Judge Paul Robert Ayers, > 70, a Mason, and the Senior Vice President of the Association of Her Majesty's District Judges, unrelentingly deviated from the truth under oath (on record)—Habakkuk 1:4, they will confirm the belief of millions of Great Britons, which is that Antichrist Charitable Freemasonry Quasi-Religion (Mediocre Mafia, New Pharisees, New Good Samaritans, Defenders of Faiths, including all the faiths and/or religions associated with the 15 Holy Books in the House of Commons, and Dissenters of the Faith—John 14:6), Antichrist Islam, Antichrist Judaism, and all other motley assemblies of exotic religions and faiths under the common umbrella of the Governor of the Church of England, and the Defender of the Faith (John 14:6)—are not intellectually flawed Satanic Mumbo Jumbo.

Based on cogent and irrefutable evidence, and very, very, proximate observations and direct experiences, their law is equal for blacks and whites, but its administration is not, and it is tyrants' tool.

"Rightful liberty is unobstructed action according to our will within limits drawn around us by the equal rights of others. I do not add 'within the limits of the law' because law is often but the tyrant's will, and always so when it violates the rights of the individual." President Thomas Jefferson

CHAPTER ONE: Apartheid by stealth. An African whistleblower

Their legal system, almost in its entirety, is based on incompetent racist lies.

BEDFORD, ENGLAND: District Judge Paul Robert Ayers, > 70, a Mason, and the Senior Vice President of the Association of Her Majesty's District Judges, 3, St Paul's Square, MK 40 1SQ, which part of Bedford County Court, 3, St Paul's Square, MK40 1SQ, was not stolen, or which part of it is the yield of the Higher IQs of your own white mother and father, or which part of it preceded SLAVERY?

OYINBO OLE; A RACIST DESCENDANT OF THIEVES - HABAKKUK.

Based on available evidence, our own money, NIGERIA (oil/gas), is by far more relevant to the economic survival of his white spouse, his white mother, his white father, and all his white children than LUTON.

Then, racist white bastards carried and sold millions of stolen poor black children of defenceless Africans, including the ancestors of Nigerians, Nigeriens, and the white children of Meghan Markle, now, greedy bastards steal our own natural resources from our own Africa, including Nigeriens' uranium and Nigerians' crude oil and gas. Unlike Putin's Russia, there are no oil wells or gas fields in Kempston, or anywhere near where the white mother and father of Bedford's District Judge Paul Robert Ayers, > 70, a Mason, and the Senior Vice President of the Association of Her Majesty's District Judges, 3, St Paul's Square, MK 40 1SQ – were born.

Facts are sacred.

"The truth allows no choice." Dr Samuel Johnson.

OYINBO OLE. AN ULTRA-RIGHTEOUS DESCENDANT OF OWNERS OF STOLEN CHILDREN OF POOR AFRICANS - HABAKKUK.

Substitution is not emancipation; it is racist fraud.

"Moderation is a virtue only among those who are thought to have found alternatives." Henry Kissinger

No brain.
Poor in natural resources.
Several continuous centuries of stealing and slavery preceded the gigantic stolen trust fund – Habakkuk.

OYINBO OLE: Ignorant descendants of THIEVES and owners of stolen human beings, including kidnapped poor black children of defenceless Africans, including the African ancestors of Meghan Markle's white children – Habakkuk.

BEDFORD, ENGLAND: District Judge Paul Robert Ayers, > 70, a Mason, and the Senior Vice President of the Association of Her Majesty's District Judges, 3, St Paul's Square, MK 40 1SQ, white man, let me tell you, it is absolutely impossible for your talent and yields of the land on which your white father and mother were born to sustain your High Standard of Living. Your white ancestors were THIEVES and owners of stolen children of defenceless Africans, including the African ancestors of Prince Harry's white children – Habakkuk.

"Those who know the least obey the best." George Farquhar

BEDFORD, ENGLAND: White man, District Judge Paul Robert Ayers, > 70, a Mason, and the Senior Vice President of the Association of Her Majesty's District Judges, 3, St Paul's Square, MK 40 1SQ, let me tell you, prior to SLAVERY, there was only subsistence feudal agriculture. You're rich ONLY because African descendants of the robbed do not, yet, have overwhelming leverage necessary to demand and extract equitable reparation. You are drowning in debt, as several centuries of unpaid interest accrue - Habakkuk.

Gigantic yields of millions of stolen poor black African children, including the African ancestors of Meghan Markle's white children, not feudal agriculture, lured Eastern European Jews to Great Britain; they followed the money.

GDC: Stephanie Twidale (TD) lied.

A RACIST CROOKED SOLDIER (TERRITORIAL DEFENCE).

The USA is NATO, and absolutely everything else is an auxiliary bluff.

Europe will fight to the last American.

******

GDC CHAMBERS, 18.11.2008:

DAVID MORRIS (BARRISTER THAT WAS INSTRUCTED BY THE MPS): Just in terms of the April 2003 visit, I think you have mentioned the Health Care Commission and you were asked to provide details of all your practice visit reports back in 2006.

RICHARD HILL (NHS): Yes.

DAVID MORRIS (BARRISTER THAT WAS INSTRUCTED BY THE MPS): At that time I think some of your inspection visit reports were missing.

RICHARD HILL (NHS): Two or three were missing. The reason was and the reason I suspect why that was missing was because we had moved office, I had moved office in 2002, 2004 and 2006 and the problem is that I work for one session a week and I am at the office quite often only once every other week; the other time I'm on the road visiting. What happens is that when there's a move, other people are responsible for putting all my files into boxes and then re-filing them at the other location simply because I'm not there.

DAVID MORRIS (BARRISTER THAT WAS INSTRUCTED BY THE MPS): So when we look at the 2003 report that we have behind tab 20, it had got lost and is it the case that this is a contemporaneous document— RICHARD HILL (NHS): Yes. DAVID MORRIS (BARRISTER THAT WAS INSTRUCTED BY THE MPS):— or might it have been a document reconstituted from memory following the loss of an earlier document?

RICHARD HILL (NHS): This would have been contemporaneous. Well, when I say contemporaneous, what I would do, without support, would be to make some notes and then complete it normally the next day. This was carried out of an evening. We try to be flexible. Most of our inspections/visits are carried out at lunch time and most practitioners are happy for that; it means that we can actually have myself and one or two PCT members of staff visit as well so that we can have, if you like, a holistic approach to the whole practice, not just seeing if people comply but trying to sort of find ways in which we can support the practitioner in the future. So it is a multifaceted approach. In this particular case, we visited in the evening because Mr Bamgbelu was finding that much more convenient. I don't know whether that was because he was at dual locations he could only make it in the evening, but we would normally do it lunch time. Unfortunately, in those circumstances you do not get any support because people finish at 5 o'clock and I go straight from practice. I finish in my practice probably mid afternoon and then I arrange for that visit to be carried out in the evening.

DAVID MORRIS (BARRISTER THAT WAS INSTRUCTED BY THE MPS): So this visit that you have documented here behind tab 20, you would have had this pro forma with you, would you?

RICHARD HILL (NHS): Yes, I would take it with me.

DAVID MORRIS (BARRISTER THAT WAS INSTRUCTED BY THE MPS): Because you now have this pro forma, would there be any need to make any notes?

RICHARD HILL (NHS): I would make sort of relevant notes which are not covered by these, sort of anything to do with dentist problems, worries, that sort of thing, concerns.

DAVID MORRIS (BARRISTER THAT WAS INSTRUCTED BY THE MPS): It is really just the date, as I said, that is a concern because Mr Bamgbelu's recollection is that on that date, 2 April 2003, certainly in the evening he would have been in his Wellingborough practice. RICHARD HILL (NHS): As I said, we cross referenced it with our database which their Contracts Manager was able to do to corroborate that date, otherwise it would have been changed on the database.

*****

Sue Gregory (OBE) implied that she was aware that Richard Hill (NHS) had made previous visits to Mr Bamgbelu's practice, but she did not have any report, which meant that the alleged reports were not in the alleged practitioners file, and as Richard Hill (NHS) must have been the source of the alleged 'History of non-compliance' that was referred to in the NHS termination statement, and he alleged that he kept contemporaneous notes, the 'HISTORY' must have been derived from the alleged contemporaneous note.

'When I undertake practice visits, I take rough notes and write up the report at a later date, usually a couple of days afterwards in order to keep the report as contemporaneous as possible.' Richard Hill (NHS), withdrawal statement of 16.10.2008.

The rough notes in the withdrawal statement of 16.10.2008 seemed to fit seamlessly with the alleged handwritten drafts in the same report, and the two seemed to corroborate the misleading statement under oath, which is that Dr Richard Hill (NHS) used handwritten drafts to create two full reports. The statement by Dr Richard Hill (NHS) was untrue.

All untrue statements are misleading.

'I would make sort of relevant notes which are not covered by these, sort of anything to do with dentist problems, worries, that sort of thing, concerns.' Richard Hill (NHS), under oath, 18.11.2008

So, Sue Gregory (OBE), John Hooper (NHS), and Charlotte Dowling Goodson (NHS) were not aware of where Richard Hill (NHS) filed or stored the alleged contemporaneous notes and pro forma reports, two or three of which got missing during two yearly NHS office moves.

Sheep posing as shepherds are leading sheep.

All sheep need leaders or shepherds.

Sue Gregory (OBE) was the cardinal of immoral and immortal confusions.

"Two or three were missing. The reason was and the reason I suspect why that was missing was because we had moved office, I had moved office in 2002, 2004 and 2006 and the problem is that I work for one session a week and I am at the office quite often only once every other week; the other time I'm on the road visiting. What happens is that when there's a move, other people are responsible for putting all my files into boxes and then re-filing them at the other location simply because I'm not there (Richard Hill [NHS], under oath, on 18.11.2008).

So, Richard Hill (NHS) had some stuff that he wrote contemporaneously, which must have included 'HISTORY' stored in NHS offices, but John Hooper (NHS), Charlotte Dowling Goodson (NHS) and the cardinal of confusions, Sue Gregory (OBE) did not know where he (Richard Hill) stored his 'HISTORY'.

At least two, but a maximum of three of his reports were missing. He was not sure of the exact number, but he suspected that the reports disappeared during the chaos of office moves, which took place every two years.

Sue Gregory (OBE) must have been aware of these two-yearly NHS office moves, and some of her own stuff might have disappeared during the chaotic fog of the alleged two-yearly NHS office moves.

Part of the problems of some privileged people is that that they are oftener oblivious to the notion of infinite reasoning power and vision, as they might have never contemplated upon the supreme power that Dr Stephen Hawking alluded to, and without clear reasoning, they baselessly believe that their huge network is fail safe.

'You cannot understand the glories of the universe without believing there is some Supreme Power behind it.' Dr Stephen Hawking

He was lynched because they (Romans/Jews) were oblivious to the notion of infinite vision and reasoning power.

'One man that has a mind and knows it can always beat ten men who haven't and don't.' - George Bernard Shaw

Actually, according to RICHARD HILL (NHS), the alleged report of his visit to Mr Bamgbelu's practice in 2003 survived the chaos of the two-yearly NHS Office moves, as it was not lost, but was hiding within NHS files, and did so for several years.

If Sue Gregory (OBE), Charlotte Dowling Goodson (NHS), and John Hooper (NHS) searched in the NHS files, which RICHARD HILL (NHS) stated, under oath, was available to them; it confirmed that they were not thorough in their search.

Sue Gregory (OBE) was the cardinal of confusion.

The standard was too low.

There is a significant decline in educational standards, and it has affected almost every part of their society.

The confusions created have victims.

"In 2006 the Healthcare Commission carried out a visit to Bedfordshire PCT and I was asked to provide all my practice visit reports. While collating this information, I noticed that some inspection reports were missing, which included an inspection of Mr Bamgbelu's practice on 02.04.2003. Around that time my department moved and it is possible that some reports had been lost during the move. I did locate some of my draft handwritten notes and referred to these to prepare my inspection report dated 22.07.2004 for MR BAMGBELU's practice which at the time, I understood to be a correct and accurate record of my inspection. Following another move to different premises, I went through some of my files and found my correct inspection report dated 02.04.2003, which is exhibited to my September 2008 statement as RWH11 (Richard Hill (NHS), withdrawal statement of 16.10.2008).

Brainless nonsense: Incompetent mendacity.

BEDFORD, ENGLAND: GDC, Freemason, Brother, Richard William Hill (NHS Postgraduate Tutor), fabricated reports and unrelentingly lied under oath – Habakkuk 1:4.

A very, very, dishonest white man.

A Racist Crooked Freemason.

Had he been black, or had the Judges been black, he would have been in trouble.

MPS/GDC: Based on available evidence, David Morris (Barrister) deviated from the truth under oath (on record) – Habakkuk 1:4

They were all white, and they us, and we know. If they could legally justify it, they will kill us, albeit hands-off.

Google: Dr Anand Kamath, Dentist.

Google: Dr Richard Bamgboye, GP

They kill foreigners, disproportionately aliens, and hands-off. Extremely wicked racist bastards.

Seemingly with tacit approval closeted white supremacist Judges, they constructively cancelled the education of Africans who disagree with them.

Closeted white supremacist bastards know how to destroy their African enemies, but they do not know how to repair the scatter-heads of their own kindred.

"The best opportunity of developing academically and emotional." Bedford's District Judge.

A brainless racist white bastard.

White skin conceals a dark black brain.

He employed his own language like a Urhobo prostitute from oil/gas rich Niger Delta — who is in Great Britain to study symmetrical eyebrow decorations.

Unlike Putin's Russia, there are no oil wells and gas fields in Northampton and where his white mother and father were born.

An ultra-righteous descendant of THIEVES and owners of stolen poor black children of defenceless Africans, including the African ancestors of Meghan Markle's white children — Habakkuk.

BEDFORD, ENGLAND: GDC, Sue Gregory, Officer of the Most Excellent Order of our Empire (OBE), unrelentingly lied under oath (on record).

A very, very, dishonest white woman.

A closeted white supremacist crooked Officer of our Empire.

If all the white Freemason Judges in Great Britain (predominantly but not exclusively white) could disprove the truth that GDC, Sue Gregory, Officer of the Most Excellent Order of our Empire (OBE), unrelentingly lied under oath (on record), and if they could disprove that MPS/GDC: David Morris (Barrister) deviated from the truth under oath (on record) – Habakkuk 1:4, and if they could disprove that GDC, Freemason, Brother, Richard William Hill (NHS

Postgraduate Tutor), fabricated reports and unrelentingly lied under oath, they will confirm the belief of scores of millions of Britons, which is that Antichrist Freemasonry Quasi-Religion (Mediocre Mafia, New Pharisees, New Good Samaritans, Defenders of Faiths, including all the faiths and religions associated with the 15 Holy Books in the House of Commons, and Dissenters of the Faith – John 14:6), Antichrist Islam, Antichrist Judaism, and all the motley assemblies of faiths and religions under the common umbrella of the Governor of the Church of England and the Defender of the Faith (John 14:6) – are not intellectually flawed Satanic Mumbo Jumbo, and they will also confirm that reasoning and vision have finite boundaries. If reasoning and vision have finite boundaries, the fellow must have lied, before Jews and Romans in the Council, when he audaciously declared that He was exceptional – John 14:6.

Ignorance is bliss.

"Ignorance, madam, pure ignorance." Dr Samuel Johnson

CHAPTER TWO: Dr Ngozi Ekweremadu

BEDFORD, ENGLAND: Our District Judge **Paul Robert Ayers**, > 70, a Mason, and the Senior Vice President of the Association of Her Majesty's District Judges, 3, St Paul's Square, MK 40 1SQ. He is verifiably semi-illiterate, unlike Putin's Russia, there are no oil wells or gas fields in LUTON and where his white mother and father were born. He is rich, and he dishonestly implied that he didn't know that the white ancestors of his white mother and father were THIEVES and owners of stolen poor black children of defenceless Africans, including the West African ancestors of Meghan Markle's white children — Habakkuk.

"I know of no evil that has ever existed, nor can imagine any evil to exist, worse than the tearing of eighty thousand persons annually from their native land, by a combination of the most civilised nations inhabiting the most enlightened part of the globe, but more especially under the sanction of the laws of that Nation which calls herself the most free and the most happy of them all." Prime Minister William Pitt the Younger.

An ignorant racist white bastard. An ultra-righteous descendant of extremely nasty and merciless racist murderers, industrial-scale professional thieves, and owners of stolen poor black children of defenceless Africans, including the African ancestors of Meghan Markle's white children.

It's their brainless and baseless birth right to be superior to all Africans, and when they realise that they are not, to conceal that truth, closeted hereditary white supremacist bastards resort to indiscreet racist criminality, and their assets are their whiteness and the certainty that Judges will be white, and their hope is that all Judges will be closeted hereditary white supremacist bastards too.

"Ethical foreign policy." Robin Cook (1946–2005).

Integrity, Friendship, Respect, and Charity: If they are as brave, and as ethical as they seem to imply, why didn't they foresee that Putin will convert the Bakhmut of our eyes to the Bakhmut of our hearts; why did they look away while Putin converted Bakhmut from bricks to rubble? There are Masons in Ukraine, albeit very, very, corrupt ones.

Skin colour is a great creation of Almighty God, but it is not the greatest.

APARTHEID BY STEALTH: They seem to have been lied to at home and at school that they are superiorly created by Almighty God, and they expect everything to be assumed in favour of the universally acknowledged irrefutably superior skin colour that the very, very, fortunate wearer neither made nor chose.

Bedford, England: District Judge **Paul Robert Ayers, > 70, a Mason, and the Senior Vice President of the Association of Her Majesty's District Judges, 3, St Paul's Square, MK 40 1SQ.** An opportunist closeted white supremacist bastard saw two holes, hypothyroidism psychosis and religious psychosis, and the hereditary racist white bastard tried to use them to destroy a Nigerian family in BEDFORD.

Oxford, England: GDC/NHS, British Soldier, Territorial Defence, Stephanie Twidale (TD), unrelentingly lied under oath — Habakkuk 1:4.

A very, very, dishonest white woman.

A racist crooked British Soldier (Territorial Defence).

The USA is NATO; absolutely everything else is an auxiliary bluff.

WHITE PRIVILEGE. OXFORD, ENGLAND: GDC/NHS, Bristol University Educated Mrs Helen Falcon, Member of the Most Excellent Order of our Empire (MBE), Former Member of the GDC Committee, Very Charitable Rotarian (Quasi-Freemason), the spouse of Mr Falcon, and the former

Postgraduate Dean, Oxford, unrelentingly lied under oath (on record) — Habakkuk 1:4.

A very, very, dishonest white woman.

A Racist Crooked Member of the Most Excellent Order of our Empire of Stolen Affluence — Habakkuk.

If there is irrefutable evidence that the white ancestors of one's white mother and father were THIEVES and owners of stolen poor black children of defenceless Africans, it will be very, very, naive not to expect RACIAL HATRED complicated by incompetent mendacity to be part of one's genetic inheritance.

OYINBO OLE: Our own Nigeria, Shell's docile cash cow since 1956.

Our own Nigerian babies with huge oil wells and gas fields near their huts eat only 1.5/day in our own Nigeria, a very, very, bellyful, closeted hereditary white supremacist white woman, GDC/NHS, Bristol University Educated Mrs Helen Falcon, Member of the Most Excellent Order of our Empire (MBE), Former Member of the GDC Committee, Very Charitable Rotarian (Quasi-Freemason), the spouse of Mr Falcon, whose white father and mother have never seen crude oil, and whose white ancestors, including the white ancestors of Winston Churchill (1874–1965) — were fed like battery hens with yields of stolen poor black children of defenceless Africans, including the African ancestors of Prince Harry's white children, was our former Postgraduate Dean, Oxford — Habakkuk.

INTELLECTUAL COWARDS: To disengage from open debates, they unilaterally declare that their African enemies — who refuse to be subservient to irrefutably physically and mentally ill-favoured human beings, with universally acknowledged superior skin colour, are lunatics, as any mere African (African Bombata) who disagrees with any member of the brainlessly and baselessly self-awarded superior race — must be a lunatic.

If there is irrefutable evidence that skin colour that one neither made nor chose is universally acknowledged to be superior, and if one's intellect is not, and if one is a crooked and incompetently dishonest closeted hereditary white supremacist bastard, it is plainly deductible that Freedom of Expression is not one's friend.

They are professional racist criminals, and they are like RATS.

Like rats, they love to act without being seen, and like rats they are excessively stupid, as they defecate everywhere leaving tell-tale signs.

Based on several decades of very, very, proximate observations and direct experiences, they are extremely nasty racist bastards, and if you can see them as they truly are, and if they know that you can see them, you have inadvertently reached the end of your life, as all loose ends must be tied by hook or by crook.

"I know of no evil that has ever existed, nor can imagine any evil to exist, worse than the tearing of eighty thousand persons annually from their native land, by a combination of the most civilised nations inhabiting the most enlightened part of the globe, but more especially under the sanction of the laws of that Nation which calls herself the most free and the most happy of them all." Prime Minister William Pitt the Younger.

Prior to slavery, there weren't very many proper houses in Bristol.

Bristol University (1876) was preceded by SLAVERY.

Before the extortionately profitable evil commerce in millions of stolen poor black African children, there was only subsistence agriculture.

"Agriculture not only gives riches to a nation, but the only one she can call her own." Dr Samuel Johnson.

They are very, very, highly civilised, and super enlightened, and they do everything, absolutely everything legally, including hereditary racial hatred and indiscreet FRAUD.

Scotland, England: GDC, Kevin Atkinson, Scottish Kev, Postgraduate Tutor, Oxford, unrelentingly lied under oath (on record) — Habakkuk 1:4.

A very, very, dishonest, racist, and crooked Scotchman. If there is irrefutable evidence that one's white Scottish ancestors were THIEVES and owners of stolen poor black children of defenceless Africans, including the African ancestors of Meghan Markle's white children, it will be very, very, naive not to expect racial hatred complicated by incompetent mendacity to be part of one's genetic inheritances.

White man, Kevin Atkinson, Scottish Kev, Postgraduate Tutor, Oxford, let me tell you, you are an ignorant racist crook, and your brain is not good. You are worthy only because you are white and England is very, very, rich? What else? Scotsman, let me tell you, your Scottish ancestors were industrial-scale professional THIEVES, extremely nasty racist murderers, and owners of stolen African children of defenceless Africans, including the African ancestors of the white children of Prince Harry.

Based on available evidence, the entire foundations of Glasgow and Edinburgh were built with bones, bones of stolen poor children of defenceless Africans, including the African ancestors of Meghan Markle's white children, and more bones than the millions of skulls at the doorstep of Comrade Pol Pot (1925–1998) — Habakkuk.

OYINBO OLE: WHITE THIEVES: HABAKKUK.

BEDFORD, ENGLAND: GDC, Freemason, Brother, Richard William Hill, NHS Postgraduate Tutor, fabricated reports and unrelentingly lied under oath – Habakkuk 1:4.

A very, very, dishonest white man.

A racist crooked descendant of ultra-righteous white thieves and owners of stolen children of defenceless poor people – Habakkuk.

Facts are sacred, and they cannot be overstated.

Bedford, England: District Judge. An opportunist closeted white supremacist bastard saw two holes, hypothyroidism psychosis and religious psychosis, and the hereditary racist white bastard tried to use them to destroy a Nigerian family in BEDFORD. Oxford, England: GDC/NHS, British Soldier, Territorial Defence, Stephanie Twidale (TD), unrelentingly lied under oath — Habakkuk 1:4. A very, very, dishonest white woman. A racist crooked British Soldier (Territorial Defence). The USA is NATO; absolutely everything else is an auxiliary bluff.

Case No: 2YL06820

Bedford County Court
May House
29 Goldington Road
Bedford
MK40 3NN

Monday, 1st July 2013

B E F O R E:

DISTRICT JUDGE AYERS

DOBERN PROPERTY LIMITED
(Claimants)

v.

DR. ABIODUN OLA BAMGBELU
(Defendant)

Transcript from an Official Court Tape Recording.
Transcript prepared by:
MK Transcribing Services
29 The Concourse, Brunel Business Centre,

Bletchley, Milton Keynes, MK2 2ES
Tel: 01908-640067 Fax: 01908-365958
DX 100031 Bletchley
Official Court Tape Transcribers.

MR. PURKIS appeared on behalf of THE CLAIMANTS.

THE DEFENDANT appeared in PERSON.

PROCEEDINGS OF MONDAY, 1ST JULY 2013

Monday, 1st July 2013

DISTRICT JUDGE AYERS: Mr. Purkis, you weren't here, I know, on the last occasion representing the claimants, but we had a very long hearing concerning the lease. There's a letter from Mr. Bamgbelu dated 6th June, which I don't know whether you have seen.

MR. PURKIS: Yes, sir.

DISTRICT JUDGE AYERS: In that case it seems to me it's over to you to prove your case.

MR. PURKIS: Sir, it continues to be our case that we rely on the lease and the terms of the lease that have been put forward. On the last occasion, my understanding was that it was – in essence it was accepted by the court that those terms were likely to be terms between the parties that were entered into, and I'm referring to the lease contained in the bundle. Mr. Bamgbelu was therefore required to dispute that, in essence, by providing a copy of a lease that he said contained the appropriate terms.

DISTRICT JUDGE AYERS: What I actually said to him, and I went through this numerous times with him, was that the copy of the lease that you produced was the one at the Land Registry, it happened to be the one signed by the landlord, and he was saying that that wasn't the one that was signed by him. He said he had solicitors at the time who advised him, and pressing very hard about it, and on numerous occasions, he insisted that he wished to go back to his solicitors then and find a copy of the lease that they had that they advised him on, and to check that against the copy that you have. The letter, as you see, simply says that he doesn't accept that, and it's up to you to produce a copy signed by him. Well, the position is very very clear this afternoon. I made a very clear order on the last occasion that if he didn't produce any evidence to challenge the validity of your lease, as your lease was registered at the Land Registry, I would accept that even if he would not be in a position to challenge what that lease contained. End of story. He is stuck with that lease. All I want to do today is to hear evidence from you as to the amount outstanding.

MR. PURKIS: Thank you, sir.

MR. BAMGBELU: Am I allowed to say something, sir?

DISTRICT JUDGE AYERS: No. Do you wish to -----

MR. BAMGBELU: It is not fair, sir.

DISTRICT JUDGE AYERS: Mr. Bamgbelu, do you wish to say anything about that particular issue?

MR. BAMGBELU: Yes, sir.

DISTRICT JUDGE AYERS: What do you wish to say?

MR. BAMGBELU: The lease that I read and signed, when you sign the lease, sir, it is exchanged. The only lease that I read and signed -----

DISTRICT JUDGE AYERS: No, Mr. Bamgbelu, let me explain this to you.

MR. BAMGBELU: That'-----

DISTRICT JUDGE AYERS: It is up to the claimants to prove their case. They have produced a copy of the lease that is registered at the Land Registry. That is a lease and they are able to prove their case on that. The fact that they have not got your copy or the copy signed by you, is neither here nor there, because the importance is the document which is registered at the Land Registry, and investigations say that it is a copy signed by the landlord which has to be placed at the Land Registry. I made that perfectly clear to you on the last occasion.

MR. BAMGBELU: That's -----

DISTRICT JUDGE AYERS: You were the one who challenged that that lease was not an accurate copy of the lease that you've signed.

MR. BAMGBELU: I did not say that, sir.

DISTRICT JUDGE AYERS: Yes, you did.

MR. BAMGBELU: I did not say that, sir.

DISTRICT JUDGE AYERS: I was here the last occasion -----

MR. BAMGBELU: I did not say that, sir.

DISTRICT JUDGE AYERS: ----- that is exactly what you said.

MR. BAMGBELU: What I said, sir, was that I am happy to accept that.

DISTRICT JUDGE AYERS: No, you weren't.

MR. BAMGBELU: I said that.

DISTRICT JUDGE AYERS: Mr. Bamgbelu, you cannot argue with me, I was here, because I was at some -----

MR. BAMGBELU: Okay.

DISTRICT JUDGE AYERS: ----- considerable length to go through that with you, because you kept saying -----

MR. BAMGBELU: I said -----

DISTRICT JUDGE AYERS: ----- that, and I said if you accept -----

MR. BAMGBELU: I accepted it, sir.

DISTRICT JUDGE AYERS: ----- if you accept that lease as the lease, then we didn't need to go any further. You insisted on having the matter adjourned so you could go -----

MR. BAMGBELU: I did not do that, sir.

DISTRICT JUDGE AYERS: ----- and get – okay.

MR. BAMGBELU: Yes.

DISTRICT JUDGE AYERS: Well, okay, we'll disagree on that then, but I can remember full well what I said -----

MR. BAMGBELU: I have a very good memory, sir.

DISTRICT JUDGE AYERS: ----- and if necessary -----

MR. BAMGBELU: As well as (Inaudible).

DISTRICT JUDGE AYERS: ----- if necessary I will have the tape played back to you -----

MR. BAMGBELU: Yes, yes.

DISTRICT JUDGE AYERS: ----- that's exactly what is said.

MR. BAMGBELU: Okay.

MR. PURKIS: The claim is for £320.66 service charge.

DISTRICT JUDGE AYERS: Well, you'd better, I think, call your client or Mrs. Thomas to give evidence, to deal with the issues that are outstanding.

MR. PURKIS: Certainly, sir. May I call Mrs. Thomas?

Mrs. L. Thomas

Examined by Mr. Purkis.

Q. Mrs. Thomas, you have a bundle in front of you, and I believe that if you turn to page 141, you'll see a document there that says at the top, 'Witness statement of Lisa Thomas.' Is that your witness statement?

A. That's correct.

Q. If we turn to paragraph 8 there, it says, 'In the circumstances, I respectfully ask the court to enter judgment for the amount claimed of £410.66,' then it says, 'which comprises of the court fee for issuing the claim, totalling £95, and solicitors fees on issuing of £80.' Can I confirm that those fees of £95 and £80 aren't in fact included in that £410.66?

A. No, there is an error.

DISTRICT JUDGE AYERS: Right. Before we go any further, Mr. Purkis, we'd better have your client telling me who she is.

MR. PURKIS: Very well, sir. Could you give your full name to the court?

A. My name is Mrs. Lisa Jane Thomas, I'm property manager for Residential Block Management Services, and our clients are Dobern Properties.

Q. And how long have you been managing this particular block?

A. From around December 2010 when we was instructed by the previous agents. They were the administrators.

MR. BAMGBELU: Do you have proof of that?

******

They were all white.

Homogeneity in the administration of English Law is the impregnable secure mask of merciless RACIST EVIL - Habakkuk 1:4; John 8:44; John 10:10.

Their system subjugates colour blind-merit and propagates Apartheid by stealth.

Based on available evidence, Our District Judge Paul Robert Ayers, > 70, a Mason, and the Senior Vice President of the Association of Her Majesty's District Judges, 3, St Paul's Square, MK 40 1SQ, maliciously lied, or he recklessly deviated from the truth, or he was pathologically confused (Alzheimer's disease)—when he explicitly stated that the Nigerian was invited to, and took part in, the hearing of July 1, 2013, at Bedford County Court, May House, 29, Goldington Road, Bedford, MK40 3NN.

The White Judge Lied.

Google: The White Judge Lied.

Based on observation and direct experiences, not all liars are racists, but all racists are malicious liars.

If there is cogent and absolutely irrefutable evidence that the white ancestors of one's white mother and father were

THIEVES and owners of stolen poor children of defenceless Africans, including the African ancestors of Meghan Markle's white children, it will be very, very, naïve, not to expect RACIAL HATRED complicated by incompetent mendacity to be part of one's genetic inheritances.

Before the RACIAL HATRED of closeted hereditary opportunist white supremacist bastards unravel, it is a conspiracy theory, and when it does, it instantly mutates to a mistake.

Based on available evidence, 29, Goldington Road, Bedford, MK40 3NN, is a block of flats.

An ignorant racist fool.

An ultra-righteous descendant of THIEVES and owners of stolen poor black children of defenceless Africans, including the African ancestors of Meghan Markle's white children – Habakkuk, sat on a very highchair that was constructed with bones of stolen poor black children of poor Africans, including the African ancestors of Prince Harry's white children, more bones of the innocent African children than the millions of skulls at the doorstep of Comrade Pol Pot (1925 – 1998) – in our Grand Cathedral Court that was preceded by SLAVERY.

Facts are sacred.

Based on available evidence, Bedford's District Judge Paul Robert Ayers, > 70, a Mason, and the Senior Vice

President of the Association of Her Majesty's District Judges, 3, St Paul's Square, MK 40 1SQ, unrelentingly deviated from the truth under oath (approved Judgement)—Habakkuk 1:4.

Alzheimer's disease is considerably more common than ordinarily realised and it is incompatible with the competent administration of English Law.

The competent administration of English Law should be an inviolable basic right.

All for one, and one for all: Their people are everywhere, and they control almost everything in Great Britain.

Based on observations and direct experiences, they are closeted hereditary white supremacist thugs.

Then, all Judges were white, and most of them were Masons, and some of them were thicker than a gross of planks.

If all the white Freemason Judges in Great Britain (predominantly but not exclusively white), including all the white 33rd Degree Freemasons, Scottish Rite (disproportionately but not exclusively white), at the Bedfordshire Masonic Centre, the Keep, Bedford Road, Kempston, MK 42 8AH (integrity, friendship, respect, and charity), could disprove the truth that District Judge Paul Robert Ayers, > 70, a Mason, and the Senior Vice President of the Association of Her Majesty's District Judges, 3, St Paul's Square, MK 40 1SQ, unrelentingly deviated from the truth under oath (approved Judgement)—Habakkuk 1:4, they will confirm the belief of scores of millions of Britons, which is that sexed-up legal transcripts do not exist in the administration of English Law, and if they could disprove the truth that GDC, Freemason, Brother, Richard William Hill (NHS Postgraduate Tutor), of Bedford, England, fabricated reports and unrelentingly lied under oath – Habakkuk 1:4, and if they could disprove the truth that GDC, Ms Sue Gregory, Officer of the Most Excellent Order of our Empire, of Bedford, England, unrelentingly lied under oath (on record)—Habakkuk 1:4, they will confirm the belief of billions of people in our world, which is that Antichrist Freemasonry Quasi-Religion (Mediocre Mafia, New Pharisees, New Good Samaritans, Defenders of Faiths, including all the Faiths associated with the 15 Holy Books in the House of Commons, and Dissenters of the Faith— John 14:6), Antichrist Islam, Antichrist Judaism, and ALL other motley assemblies of exotic religions and faiths, under the common umbrella of the Governor of the Church of England, and the Defender of the Faith (John 14:6)—are not intellectually flawed Satanic Mumbo Jumbo, and they will also confirm that reasoning and vision have finite boundaries. If Charitable Freemasons (Dissenters of the Faith—John 14.6) could prove that reasoning and vision have finite boundaries, they will concomitantly confirm the belief of Dissenters of the Faith—John 14:6, which is that the fellow lied or He was thoroughly confused when, before Jews and Romans, in the Council, He disclosed pictures His unbounded mind painted, and He must have also lied when He audaciously stated:

"I am the way and the truth and the life. No one comes to the Father except through me" (John 14:6).

"The first quality that is needed is audacity." Sir Winston Churchill (1874–1975).

If the fellow told the truth, in the Council, before Jews and Romans, we are all FORKED, and His Knights attack Kings and Queens simultaneously, and only Queens can escape, so it is CHECKMATE, and everything that is not aligned with the notion of His infinite reasoning and vision (John 14:6) - is fu*ked.

Jews and Romans lynched the fellow like Gadhafi, and He was crucified only He spoke. Our own Messiah was not punished for speaking, He was lynched like Gadhafi and crucified solely to prevent Him from speaking.

"Freedom of expression is a basic right."

"It does no harm to throw the occasional man overboard, but it does not do much good if you are steering full speed ahead for the rocks." Sir Ian Gilmour (1926–2007).

CHAPTER THREE: Apartheid by stealth. An African whistle blower.

WHITE PRIVILEGE: Any African who disagrees with members of the brainlessly and baselessly self-awarded superior race is a lunatic.

The stereotypical African is a lunatic brute.

"The European knows and he does not know. On the level of reflection, a Negro is a Negro, but in the unconscious, there is a firmly fixed image of the nigger-savage." Dr Frantz Fanon

Ignorant descendants of THIEVES and owners of stolen children of defenceless poor people, including the African ancestors of Meghan Markle's white children — Habakkuk.

They hate Africans, and they look down on our people, but they will tolerate subservient Africans and Born-Again Christian Africans.

Christian belief, European civilisation, and European Laws based on Christian belief existed during several continuous centuries of merciless barbarously racist traffic in millions of stolen poor black children of defenceless Africans — Habakkuk.

GDC, 37 Wimpole St, London W1G 8DQ: Jonathan Martin, unrelentingly lied on record- Habakkuk 1:4.

A very, very, dishonest white man.

Poly-educated crooked Freemasons' Zombie.

Facts are sacred.

"The truth allows no choice." Dr Samuel Johnson

WHITE SUPREMACY: They are brainless racist white criminals, and the fact that they are white, and their people oversee the administration of their law is their most important leverage.

They know how to deal with 'culturally inferior' Africans, but they don't know how to repair the scatter-heads of their own 'culturally superior' white kindred.

They purportedly do everything, absolutely everything, legally, including racial hatred and fraud.

Northampton, England: GDC, Geraint Evans, NHS, Postgraduate Tutor, Oxford, of Rowtree Road, Northampton NN4 0NY, unrelentingly lied under oath (on record) — Habakkuk.

"They may not have been well written from a grammatical point of view ...." Geraint Evans.

An ignorant scatter-head Welsh imbecile.

Everything is assumed in favour of the universally acknowledged irrefutably superior skin colour that the very, very, fortunate wearer neither made nor chose.

Nigerian babies with huge oil wells and gas fields near their huts eat only 1.5/day in our own Nigeria, a very, very, bellyful Welsh imbecile whose white Welsh mother and father have never seen crude oil, and whose white Welsh ancestors, including the white Welsh ancestors of Aneurin

Bevan (1897–1960), were fed like battery hens with yields of stolen poor black children of defenceless Africans, including the African ancestors of the white great grandchildren of Prince Phillip (1921–2021), thrives in Great Britain, what's great about that?

Aneurin Bevan's NHS was preceded by Slavery; it paid for it.

BEDFORD, ENGLAND: District Judge **Paul Robert Ayers, > 70, a Mason, and the Senior Vice President of the Association of Her Majesty's District Judges, of 3, St Paul's Square, MK 40 1SQ,** based on very, very, proximate observations and direct experiences, you're worthy only because skin colour that you neither made nor chose is universally acknowledged to be irrefutably superior and England is very, very, rich; what else? The affluence that you implicitly brag about was preceded by Slavery; then, it was stolen with guns — Habakkuk. You are guilty, certainly, by heritage, because the white ancestors of your white mother and father were industrial-scale professional thieves and owners of stolen poor black children of defenceless poor people, including the African ancestors of the white children of Meghan Markle — Habakkuk.

It is plainly deductible that properly rehearsed ultra-righteousness and deceptively schooled higher civilisation — were preceded by several continuous centuries of merciless racist evil: The greediest economic cannibalism and the evilest racist terrorism the world will ever know Habakkuk.

It is absolutely impossible for your Christ-given talent and yields of the land on which your own white father and mother were born to sustain your relatively higher standard of living.

BEDFORD, ENGLAND: District Judge Paul Robert Ayers, > 70: a Mason, and the Senior Vice President of the Association of Her Majesty's District Judges, of 3, St Paul's Square, MK 40 1SQ, It is the absolute truth, supported by cogent facts and irrefutable evidence — that Nigeria (oil/gas) is by far more relevant to the economic survival of your white mother and father, your white spouse, and all your white children than Kempston.

Unlike Putin's Russia, there are no oil wells or gas fields in LUTON, and where your own white father and mother were born.

The very, very, highly luxuriant soil of Northamptonshire yields only food, and unlike Niger, there are no uranium mines in Bishop's Stortford. Bishop's Stortford's Cecil Rhodes (1853 – 1902) was a racist white bastard and a THIEF – Habakkuk.

"We shall deal with the racist bastards when we get out of prison." Robert Mugabe (1924 – 2019).

Perception is grander than reality.

Like our universe, affluence did not evolve from NOTHING.

Then, almost everything was actively and deliberately stolen with guns — Habakkuk.

"Affluence is not a birth right." David Cameron.

Before Slavery, what?

Then, there was only subsistence feudal agriculture.

"Agriculture not only gives riches to a nation, but the only one she can call her own." Dr Samuel Johnson.

Ignorance is bliss.

Facts are sacred, and they cannot be overstated.

They, unrelentingly, tell incompetent racist lies, including under oath, and they overwhelm the minds of some foreigners, with incompetent racist mendacity, and they kill them, albeit hands-off, and they get very, very, angry when they realise that Africans know that we, like our ancestors, remain inferior to members of the brainlessly and baselessly self-awarded superior race, irrespective of our Christ granted talents, and particular under the administration of their indiscreetly institutionally law.

Crude and cruel white supremacist bastards systematically killed Dr Richard Bamgboye, GP, and Dr Anand Kamath, Dentist, albeit hands-off.

They, foreigners, Dr Richard Bamgboye, GP (Nigerian), and Dr Anand Kamath, Dentist (Indian), came to Great Britain for better life, closeted hereditary white supremacist bastards overwhelmed their minds with unrelenting incompetent racist lies, and prematurely sent them to afterlife.

Dr Richard Bamgboye, GP, and Dr Anand Kamath, Dentist, we will come to you, for you will never return to us – 2 Samuel 12:23.

NORTHAMPTON, ENGLAND: GDC, Ms Rachael Bishop, Senior NHS Nurse, unrelentingly lied under oath – Habakuk 1:4.

A very, very, dishonest white woman.

'She is a typical English woman, usually dull and always violent.' Sebastian Melmoth paraphrased.

NORTHAMPTON, ENGLAND: GDC, Ms Rachael Bishop, Senior NHS Nurse, a crooked, closeted hereditary racist, and incompetently dishonest Senior NHS Nurse of our Empire of Stolen Affluence - Habakkuk

Closeted hereditary white supremacist bastards persecute our people (Africans) for the dark coat that we neither made nor chose, and they steal yields of our Christ granted talents, and they impede our ascent from the bottomless crater into which their insatiably greedy and racist ancestors (bastards) threw ours, in the African bush, unprovoked, during several continuous centuries of merciless racist evil — Habakkuk.

Equitably just reparation pends, and several continuous centuries of unpaid interest accrue - Habakkuk.

Based on several decades of very, very, proximate observations and direct experiences, they are extremely wicked people, and the hatred they have for black people is unnatural and illogical.

"The white man is the devil." Mohammed Ali (1942–2016).

Based on several decades of very, very, proximate observations and direct experiences, the white man is not only the devil, but he is also a THIEF (Oyinbo Ole) — Habakkuk.

Closeted, hereditary white supremacist bastards do everything, absolutely everything, legally, including racial hatred and fraud — Habakkuk 1:4.

BEDFORD, ENGLAND: Based on available evidence, GDC, Sue Gregory, Officer of the Most Excellent Order of our Empire (OBE), unrelentingly lied under oath (on record) — Habakkuk 1:4.

White Privilege: Their legal system is indiscreetly dishonest, crooked, and institutionally racist, and it allows white people, only white people, to tell lies under oath (on record) — Habakkuk 1:4.

Ignorant, very, very, shallow racist bastards: Before uncontrollable hereditary racial hatred unravels, it is a conspiracy theory, and when it does, it instantly mutates to a mistake.

"The supreme vice is shallowness." Wilde.

Based on several continuous decades of very, very, proximate observations and direct experiences, the administration of their law is a very, very, potent weapon of race war.

They know how to destroy Africans by covering up the crookedness and racial hatred of their own white kindred — Habakkuk 1:4.

GDC, Sue Gregory (OBE): A racist crooked Officer of the Most Excellent Order of our Empire of Stolen Affluence — Habakkuk.

White Privilege: Had Sue Gregory (OBE), the racist crooked Officer of the Most Excellent Order of our Empire of Stolen Affluence — been black, or had the Judges been black, she would have been in trouble — Habakkuk 1:4.

"Michael Jackson would have been found guilty if he'd black." Jo Brand.

Like our universe, our Empire did not evolve from NOTHING, then, almost everything was actively and deliberately stolen with guns — Habakkuk.

Then, in pursuant of concealing intellectual impotence and uncontrollable hereditary racial intolerance, they adorned crooked racist white bastards (predominantly but not exclusively white) with very, very high titles, and they became Freemasons' Zombie Private Soldiers — Habakkuk 1:4.

OXFORD, ENGLAND: GDC, Bristol University Educated Mrs Helen Falcon, Member of the Most Excellent Order of our Empire (MBE), a former Member of the GDC Committee, a selfless Rotarian (Quasi-Mason), a former

Postgraduate Dean, Oxford, and the spouse of Mr Falcon, unrelentingly lied under oath (on record) — Habakkuk 1:4.

White Privilege: A very, very, dishonest privileged white woman.

An indiscreetly crooked and hereditary racist Member of the Most Excellent Order of our Empire of Stolen Affluence — Habakkuk.

The crooked hereditary racist white woman, Member of the Most Excellent Order of our Empire of Stolen Affluence — reminded one of very coarse and ugly Welsh wenches a poet encountered.

"The ordinary women of Wales are generally short and squat, ill-favoured, and nasty." David Mallet (1705–1765).

The truth does not favour hereditary racist bastards, so they unilaterally declare that their African victims are lunatic, when the only truth is that they are intellectually impotent incompetent racist liars.

They hate us, and we know.

They fear untamed minds of self-educated Africans more than Putin's poisons.

Based on cogent, irrefutable, and available evidence, the entire foundation of Bristol, including Bristol University, where Mrs Helen Falcon (MBE) was a student, was constructed with bones, bones of stolen poor black children of defenceless Africans, including the African ancestors of Meghan Markle's white children, and more bones than the millions of skulls at the doorstep of Comrade Pol Pot (1925–1998).

Google: Helen Falcon, Racist Empress.

Putin does not want Zelensky and Ukrainians to be part of our very, very highly civilised, super enlightened, and very, very, Free World, where a crooked racist white cougar, Mrs Helen Falcon, MBE, is a Member of the Most Excellent Order of our Empire of Stolen Affluence, and where a crooked racist white cougar, Sue Gregory, OBE, is an Officer of the Most Excellent Order of our Empire of Stolen Affluence, so he converted Bakhmut of our eyes to Bakhmut of our hearts,

Bakhmut's bricks are now rubble.

Sometimes privileged white dullards hate to hear the truth, especially from mere Africans (African Bombata).

Anyone, particularly a mere African — who disagrees with members of the brainlessly and baselessly self-awarded superior race must be a lunatic.

"To disagree with three — fourths of the British public on all points is one of the first elements of sanity, one of the deepest consolations in all moments of spiritual doubt." Wilde.

Deluded and conceited ignorant racist shallow fools.

Was Christ a lunatic or was a He a liar.

One dimensionally educated intellectually impotent racist rubbish see molecules and they destroy all self-educated Africans who see quarks — because they are too stupid to discern the truth, which is that reasoning and vision have no finite boundaries.

Rather than admit that intellect has absolutely NOTHING to do with their universally acknowledged irrefutably superior skin colour, which they neither made nor chose, they resort to racist criminality guarded and guided by incompetent mendacity, and Negrophobic Perjury guards and guides incompetent Persecutory Negrophobia, and their safety net is the certainty that Judges will always be white, and their hope is that Judges will be racist white bastards too.

BEDFORD, ENGLAND: District Judge Paul Robert Ayers, a Mason, > 70, and the Senior Vice President of the Association of Her Majesty's District Judges, of 3, St, Paul's Square, MK40 1SQ, the mind that the Negro got is finer than your system, and it is possible to irreversibly destroy you and it with cogent facts and irrefutable evidence.

Their irreparably mediocre, vindictive, indiscreetly dishonest, potently weaponised, and institutionally racist legal system — Habakkuk 1:4.

White criminals and white Judges seem to work as a team, and their common interest is the continuing propagation of their indiscreetly white supremacist and institutionally racist legal system.

We disagree, and irreconcilably.

"Sometimes people do not want to hear the truth because they don't want their illusions destroyed." Friedrich Nietzsche.

"Hello, this is Bing. I searched for "judge ayers bedford" and found some results that might be relevant to your query. According to the results, District Judge Paul Robert Ayers is a judge at the Bedford County Court in Bedfordshire, England1. He is also the Senior Vice President of the Association of Her Majesty's District Judges2. However, most of the results are from books or posts that accuse him of being a racist, a liar, a Freemason, and a descendant of thieves and murderers132456. These claims are made by a Nigerian author named Michael Coleade, who seems to have a personal vendetta against Judge Ayers and other officials in Bedford32456. I cannot verify the accuracy or validity of these accusations, as they are based on the author's opinions and experiences. You may want to do further research or consult other sources before forming your own judgment. Is there anything else I can help you with?

Yes.

What is the meaning of 'however', and what is its relevance, and why isn't it a bloody waste of word?

If Bing could disprove the truth that Bedford's District Judge unrelentingly deviated from the truth under oath (approved judgement), they will confirm the belief of billions of people in our world, which is that Antichrist Freemasonry Quasi-Religion (Mediocre Mafia, New Pharisees, New Good Samaritans, Defenders of Faiths, including all the exotic faiths and religions associated with the 15 Holy Books in the House of Commons, and Dissenters of the faith — John 14:6), Antichrist Islam, Antichrist Judaism, and all other motley assemblies of exotic religions and faiths, under the common umbrella of the Governor of the Church of England and the Defender of the Faith — John 14:6, are intellectually flawed Satanic Mumbo Jumbo, and they will concomitantly confirm that reasoning and vision have finite boundaries, and if reasoning and vision have finite boundaries, the fellow must have lied, before Jews, and Romans, when He purportedly disclosed pictures His unbounded mind painted, and He must have lied when He audaciously and expressly declared that He was exceptional — John 14:6.

Facebook. https://www.facebook.com/Daringtruths01/p…Da ringtruths — DISTRICT JUDGE AYERS OF BEDFORD …

WebDISTRICT JUDGE PAUL AYERS: Based on observations, a RACIST descendant of RACISTS, MURDERERS, DRUG DEALERS (OPIUM), PROFESSIONAL THIEVES, and owners of STOLEN HUMAN BEINGS.

CHAPTER FOUR: Dr Ngozi Ekweremadu.

BEDFORD, ENGLAND: District Judge Paul Robert Ayers, a Mason, > 70, and the Senior Vice President of the Association of Her Majesty's District Judges, of 3, St, Paul's Square, MK40 1SQ, what do you own that is tangible that wasn't STOLEN, or is the yield of transparent virtue, or preceded SLAVERY?

An ignorant descendant of THIEVES and owners of stolen children of defenceless AFRICANS, including the West African ancestors of the white great grandchildren of Prince Phillip (1921–2021).

Philippians 1:21: Was Phillip a Mason?

GDC: Sue Gregory (OBE) lied.

A Racist Crooked OBE.

Closeted hereditary white supremacist bastards saw two holes, hypothyroidism psychosis and religious psychosis, and they're trying to use those weak points to destroy innocent black African children, which descendants of carrier and sellers of stolen African children deceptively purport to seek to protect, and psychologically and intellectually insecure white supremacist bastards are working very hard to destroy the children's Nigerian dad, remove their natural shield, and impose an alien educationally inferior culture on Nigerian children.

Closeted hereditary white supremacist bastards brainlessly and basely awarded themselves supreme knowledge, and they vindictively destroy all self-educated Nigerians who disagree with them, and as they are very, very, highly civilised and super-enlightened, they do everything, absolutely everything, legally, albeit within the parameters of their indiscreetly institutionally racist legal system.

"He is an Englishman, usually violent and always dull." Wilde.

If there is cogent and irrefutable evidence that the white ancestors of one's white mother and father were THIEVES and owners of stolen poor black children of defenceless Africans, including the African ancestors of the white great grandchildren of Prince Phillip (1921–2021), it will be very, very, naive not to expect hereditary racial hatred complicated by incompetent racist mendacity to be part of one's genetic inheritances — Habakkuk.

Ignorant closeted hereditary white supremacist bastards see molecules, and motivated by uncontrollable racial hatred and envy, they vindictively destroy all self-educated Nigerians who see quarks.

https://www.youtube.com/watch?v=BlpH4hG7m1A.

Based on available evidence, our impartial Judge is a functional semi-illiterate and an incompetent liar: A closeted hereditary white supremacist descendant of THIEVES and owners of stolen poor black children of defenceless Africans, including the African ancestors of Meghan Markle's white children - Habakkuk.

Facts are sacred.

Then, for their legal system to work as designed they must have SUPREME KNOWLEDGE, but they didn't, so they criminally destroyed Nigerians who secretly looked down on their crooked mediocre intellect – Habakkuk 1:4.

Then, it was a crime and illegal only if Freemasons did not prior authorise it, and when their crooked closeted hereditary white supremacist kindred commit racist crimes against our people, closeted hereditary white supremacist Judges, the principal beneficiaries of their indiscreetly institutionally racist legal system become the chief counsels for racist white criminals, and furthermore, in pursuant of concealing crookedness and racial hatred, they adorn crooks and racist bastards very, very, high titles: They are GUILTY, and the only transparently just Judge, is transparently just because He knows all, and He sees all – Proverbs 15:3, John 5:22.

Then, without measurable objectivity, they deceived their own mentally gentler children that they are geniuses, and they vindictively destroyed all Nigerians who knew that they were not.

Skin colour is a great creation of Almighty God, but it is not the greatest.

Skin colour, not the more progressive God granted colour-blind intellect or wisdom (Proverbs 3), was the sole basis of segregation, Apartheid, white privilege, and white supremacy.

Intellect is the greatest creation of Almighty God, and it has absolutely nothing to do with the universally acknowledged irrefutably superior skin colour that the very, very, fortunate wearer neither made nor chose.

Motivated by uncontrollable racial hatred and envy, they vindictively constructively cancelled the education of self-educated Nigerians who disagree with them and with it, our livelihood, and they stole yields of our Christ granted talents, and they impede our ascent from the bottomless crater into which their extremely nasty and insatiably greedy ancestors threw ours in the African bush, unprovoked, during several continuous centuries of the greediest economic cannibalism and the evilest racist terrorism the world will ever know – Habakkuk. Then, racist bastards were greedier than the grave, and like death, they were never satisfied — Habakkuk 2:5.

Facts are sacred, and they cannot be overstated.

"The truth allows no choice." Dr Samuel Johnson

This, and only this, is the truth: Then, they were absolutely unplayable, and the weapon of the direct descendants of the father of lies (John 8:44) was the mother of all racist lies, and their power was the certainty that all Judges will be white, and the hope of hereditary closeted white supremacist bastards was that all Judges will be closeted hereditary white supremacist bastards too – Habakkuk 1:4.

Then, there was no law, as the law was what Freemasons wanted, and verdicts were prior agreed in Freemasons' Temples, and in the open courts, incompetent art incompetently imitated life — Habakkuk 1:4.

Based on cogent, irrefutable, and available evidence, then, to conceal the irrefutable exceptionalism of genetic Nigerians, closeted hereditary white supremacist bastards resorted to Negrophobic Judicial Terrorism.

Exceedingly Charitable, Ultra-righteous, and Divinely Selfless Closeted Hereditary White Supremacist Freemasons (Mediocre Mafia, New Pharisees, New Good Samaritans, Defenders of Faiths, including Faiths associated with the 15 Holy Books in the House of Commons, and Dissenters of the

Faith – John 14:6): Their people are everywhere, and they control almost everything, and they hate us (Nigerians), and we know – Habakkuk 1:4.

BEDFORD, ENGLAND: GDC, seemingly with the prior approval of Charitable Freemasons, as most things are, and as it is a crime only if Charitable Freemasons did not prior authorise it, Freemason, Brother, Richard William Hill (NHS Postgraduate Tutor) fabricated reports and unrelentingly lied under oath – Habakkuk 1:4.

A very, very, dishonest white man.

A racist crooked NHS postgraduate tutor of our Empire of Stolen Affluence — Habakkuk.

WHITE PRIVILEGE: He is very, very, lucky that he is white. Had he been black, or had the Judges been black, he would have been in trouble – Habakkuk 1:4.

President Zelensky, the ruler of the poorest country in Europe wants President Biden, the ruler of the richest country on earth to send the sons and daughters of the richest people on earth to sacrifice their lives for the children of relative paupers, the professional comedian must believe another American President:

"All men are created equal." President Abraham Lincoln (1809–1865).

Brainless nonsense.

"We know all men are not created equal in the sense some people would have us believe- some people are smarter than others, some people have more opportunity because they're born with it, some men make more money than others, some ladies make better cakes than others- some people are born gifted beyond the normal scope of men. But there is one way in this country in which all men are created equal- there is one human institution that makes a pauper the equal of a Rockefeller, the stupid man the equal of an Einstein, and the ignorant man the equal of any college president. That institution, gentlemen, is a court." Harper Lee (1926–2016).

Genetic Nigerians in Great Britain: My people, my people, if you believe that you are equal to them under their law, engage it, and seek redress within it, but if you are smart and know that like your ancestors, you are inferior to them under their law, avoid them, and where it is impossible to, accept injustice, and turn the other cheek — Matthew 5: 38–48, as there is a superior, and truly transparent Justice by a colour-blind Judge, and they are not deterred by His Justice because they do not believe in His Divine Exceptionalism – John 5:22, John 14:6.

The only true Judge, is actively Judging all, including crooked closeted hereditary white supremacist Judges, with the sword of transparent truth, not Jonathan Aitken's sword of truth, as He knows all because He sees all — Proverbs 15:3, John 5:22, John 14:6.

He was born of a woman, but gifted beyond the normal scope of men, and His reasoning and vision are unbounded.

He saw quarks, and psychologically and intellectually insecure, and very, very, intolerant ignorant bastards saw molecules, so they believed He was a liar and/or a lunatic, and they lynched Him like Gadhafi, and they crucified Him only because He spoke, but they did not punish Him because He spoke what they hated, they killed Him solely to prevent Him from speaking – Matthew 27: 34- 35.

The white man should use his intellect for the benefit of his own white children in the same way as his white mother and father used their intellects for his benefit.

If the white man believes that his white father and mother did a good job with his education, it is the conclusive proof that he and his white father and mother did not know any better.

"The best opportunity of developing academically and emotional." Bedford's District Judge Paul Robert Ayers, >

70, a Mason, and the Senior Vice President of Her Majesty District Judges, 3, St Paul's Square, MK 40 1SQ.

OUR INCONTROVERTIBLY FUNCTIONAL SEMI-ILLITERATE RACIST WHITE DUNCE.

Our own Nigeria: Shell's docile cash cow since 1956.

Our bellyful incontrovertibly functional semi-illiterate former debt-collector Solicitor in Norwich (a mere former 5th rate partner) whose white father and mother have never seen crude oil, and whose white ancestors including ultra-righteous John Bunyan (1628–1688) were fed like battery hens with yields of stolen poor black African children of defenceless Africans, including the African ancestors of Meghan Markle's white children — was our District Judge in Bedford - Habakkuk

CHAPTER FIVE: Apartheid by stealth. An African whistleblower

True Nigerians in the diaspora should be able to detect when privileged dullards are talking nonsense, if they can't, they're fake Nigerians.

OXFORD, ENGLAND: GDC, Stephanie Twidale (TD) unrelentingly lied under oath—Habakkuk 1:4.

A very, very, dishonest white woman.

A racist descendant of ultra-righteous white thieves and owners of stolen poor black children of defenceless Africans, including the Nigerian ancestors of Meghan Markle's white children.

Incompetent mendacity like excessive stupidity is hereditary.

The white ancestors of her white father and mother were incompetent racist liars too, they were THIEVES and owners of stolen children of poor people.

"Those who have robbed have also lied." Dr Samuel Johnson.

If there is absolutely irrefutable evidence that the white ancestors of the white mother and father of GDC, Stephanie Twidale (TD) were THIEVES and owners of stolen children of defenceless poor Africans, it will be very, very, naive not to expect racial hatred complicated by incompetent mendacity to be part of one's genetic inheritances—Habakkuk.

"Gentlemen, you are now about to embark on a course of studies which will occupy you for two years. Together, they form a noble adventure. But I would like to remind you of an important point. Nothing that you will learn in the course of your studies will be of the slightest possible use to you in after life, save only this, that if you work hard and intelligently you should be able to detect when a man is talking rot, and that, in my view, is the main, if not the sole, purpose of education." John Alexander Smith (1863–1939), Jowett Lecturer of philosophy at Balliol College, Oxford from 1896 to 1910, and Waynflete Professor of Moral and Metaphysical Philosophy, carrying a Fellowship at Magdalen College in the same university, from 1910 to 1936.

CHECKMATE: Those we must report closeted hereditary racist white bastards to are closeted hereditary racist white bastards too, so head or tail, we lose.

BEDFORD, ENGLAND: District Judge Paul Robert Ayers, > 70, a Mason, and the Senior Vice President of Her Majesty District Judges, 3, St Paul's Square, MK 40 1SQ, based on available evidence, the white ancestors of your white mother and father were THIEVES and owners of stolen children of defenceless Africans, including the African ancestors of the white great grandchildren of HM (1926–2022).

"Mr Bamgbelu clearly has very, very strong views about education and I understand those views are based upon the fact that he is a successful dentist here in Bedford which he attributes to the fact that his parents cared for him and his education when he was young. They ensured that he had a proper fee paying education………." Bedford's District Judge Paul Robert Ayers, > 70, a Mason, and the Senior Vice President of Her Majesty District Judges, 3, St Paul's Square, MK 40 1SQ, – proofed and approved Judgement

Idiotic brainless nonsense.

"Yes, Sir, it does her honour, but it would do nobody else honour. I have indeed, not read it all. But when I take up the end of a web, and find it packthread, I do not expect, by looking further, to find embroidery." Dr Samuel Johnson

"Envy is weak." Yul Brynner

Envy is a thief.

Financial disclosure in a divorce: 'How can a mere Negro have what I don't have?'

Then, when siblings, hereditary racial hatred, and uncontrollable envy, engaged in incestuous coitus, loads of it, insanity was their offspring.

"To disagree with three—fourths of the British public on all points is one of the first elements of sanity, one of the deepest consolations in all moments of spiritual doubt." Wilde.

OYINBO OLE: Why should the white mother and father of Bedford's District Judge Paul Robert Ayers, > 70, a Mason, and the Senior Vice President of Her Majesty District Judges, 3, St Paul's Square, MK 40 1SQ, need very, very, strong views about education when there is cogent, irrefutable, and available evidence that the white ancestors of his white mother and father were INDUSTRIAL-SCALE PROFESSIONAL THIEVES and owners of stolen poor black children of defenceless Africans, including the African ancestors of Meghan Markle's white children - Habakkuk, and they left him a huge trust fund, the yield of several continuous centuries of merciless racist evil (thievery and slavery): The greediest economic cannibalism and the evilest racist terrorism the world will ever know – Habakkuk?.

OYINBO OLE: An ignorant descendant of THIEVES and owners of stolen poor black children of defenceless Africans, including the African ancestors of Meghan Markle's white children – Habakkuk.

Facts are sacred, and they cannot be overstated.

Then, and now, unipolar psychotic power drunk bastards expect all Nigerians to love them unconditionally and say only what they love to hear; deluded racist bastards should acquire dogs and/or cats.

Then, they knew how to use guns to steal for their people (slavery), but they did not know how to repair indiscreet crookedness and scatter-heads among their own people - Habakkuk.

Had they been black, or had the Judges been black, the verifiably crooked and closeted hereditary white supremacist bastards would have been in trouble – Habakkuk 1:4.

They are not our creator, but they seem unhappy that we are created.

They hate us, and we know, and they steal yields of Christ granted talents, and their safety net is the fact their kindred oversee the administration of their law, and they do everything legally, including racial hatred and fraud – Habakkuk 1:4.

It is absolutely impossible for all the Freemason Judges in Great Britain, and in the world to disprove the truth that GDC, Sue Gregory, OBE, unrelentingly lied under oath (on record) — Habakkuk 1:4.

A very, very, dishonest white woman.

OYINBO OLE: A Racist Crooked Officer of the Most
Excellent Order of our Empire of Stolen Affluence –
Habakkuk.

If all the Officers of the Most Excellent Order of our Empire
could disprove the truth that another Officer of the Most
Excellent Order of our Empire, Sue Gregory, OBE,
unrelentingly lied under oath (on record) — Habakkuk 1:4,
they will confirm the belief of billions of people in our
world, which is that Charitable Antichrist Freemasonry
Quasi-Religion (Mediocre Mafia, New Pharisees, New Good
Samaritans, Defenders of Faiths, including all the Faiths
and/or Religions associated with the 15 Holy Books in the
House of Commons, and Dissenters of the Faith — John
14:6), Antichrist Islam, Antichrist Judaism, and all other
motley assemblies of Religions and Faiths under the
Common Umbrella of the Governor of the Church of
England, and the Defender of the Faith — John 14:6, are not
intellectually flawed Satanic Mumbo Jumbo, and they will
also confirm that reasoning and vision have finite
boundaries, and if reasoning and vision have finite
boundaries, the fellow must have been dishonest, before the
Council, when He purportedly disclosed pictures His infinite
mind painted, and He must have lied when He audaciously
declared that He is extra-terrestrial, exceptional, and
immortal — John 14:6.

If the fellow told Jews and Romans the truth in the Council,
we are FORKED, all of us, as His Knights attack all Kings
and Queens simultaneously, and only the Queens can move,

and everything, absolutely everything that is not aligned with His Divine Exceptionalism (John 5:22, John 14:6) is travelling in the wrong direction and heading straight for the ROCKS.

It does no harm to throw the occasional man overboard, but it does not do much good if you are steering full speed ahead for the rocks." Sir Ian Gilmour (1926–2007).

"Those who know the least obey the best." George Farquhar

Ignorance is bliss.

"I do not approve of anything that tampers with natural ignorance. Ignorance is like a delicate exotic fruit; touch it and the bloom is gone. The whole theory of modern education is radically unsound. Fortunately, in England, at any rate, education produces no effect whatsoever. If it did, it would prove a serious danger to the upper classes, and probably lead to acts of violence in Grosvenor Square." Wilde

CHAPTER SIX: Dr Ngozi Ekweremadu

The brainless racist white bastard should use his brain for the benefit of all his own white children in the same way as his white mother and father used theirs for him.

An ignorant racist white bastard.

An ultra-righteous descendant of THIEVES and owners of stolen children of defenceless Africans, including the black ancestors of Meghan Markle's white children—Habakkuk.

They hate us, and we know. Motivated by uncontrollable racial hatred, they saw two holes, hypothyroidism psychosis and religious psychosis, and they placed the child at her exclusive mercy, and they maliciously imposed stereotypically black learning disability education on the unfortunate child, without the consent of his Nigerian father, and in court, the white District Judge disparaged the black child, and implied that statistics showed that black African boys are generally mentally inferiorly created by Almighty God.

The hereditary white supremacist bastard did not specify the statistics and/or researches he relied on.

"By definition therefore there needs to be a contact order for Mr B so that he knows when he is going to see his son. It is absolutely essential that this occurs and mother agrees with that. She said so several times in her evidence. Mrs

Waller agreed that not only should a child have the opportunity of developing relationship with both parents, any sibling should also be there so that inter- sibling relationship could be fostered and nurtured. Obviously in this particular case the children reside in different places. That immediately puts a strain on the children having limited contact with each other. F's sister is very much older than him and she will be further advanced into her adult life. Thus it is not a matter that that sibling relationship can only be fostered by the children being together. Indeed as we all know absence sometimes makes the heart grow fonder. F should have an opportunity of seeing his sister. Wherever he does that it should be done in a friendly and loving environment. If the time comes that his sister goes to university of course his contact with her will be restricted to the time that she is home from university. In years to come when they have both grown up, with their own family they will see less of each other. But it doesn't mean that they don't still love and adore each other as much as they would if they saw each other every day." The Senior Vice President of the Association of Her Majesty's District Judges—proofed and approved Judgement.

Brainless nonsense.

A very, very, stupid white man.

"There is no sin except stupidity." Wilde

"I don't want to talk grammar. I want to talk like a lady." George Bernard Shaw.

An ignorant white fool: Immortal brainless nonsense.

SHOCKING!

"Why, that is, because, dearest you are a dunce." Dr Samuel Johnson

SHOCK KING!

A functional semi-illiterate brainless racist white bastard reasoned like an imbecile (an adult with the basic skills of a child), and the white man, albeit England's class Senior Judge, expressed his reasoning worse than an imbecile.

An ultra-righteous descendant of WHITE THIEVES: Extremely nasty, vicious, and merciless racist murderers, industrial-scale professional armed robbers, armed land grabbers, gun runners, opium merchants, and owners of stolen poor black children of defenceless Africans, including the African ancestors of Meghan Markle's white children—Habakkuk.

All functional semi-illiterate white supremacist Freemason Judges are RACISTS.

Brainless and baseless self-awarded superiority is their birth right, and any Negro that challenges the centuries-old racist scam will be dealt with.

Their hairs stand on end when they are challenged by self-educated Africans.

We and our type are the ones RACIST BASTARDS will beat up without the support of the YANKS.

A CLOSETED RACIST WHITE DUNCE.

His white mother and father did not have very, very, strong views about education, had they, they would have told him that there are very, very, many cultures in our Commonwealth, including cultures from the West African bush.

"Pardon him Theodotus: 'He is a Barbarian and thinks the culture of his tribe and Island are the laws of nature." George Bernard Shaw.

Bedford's District Judge Paul Robert Ayers, .70, a Mason, and the Senior Vice President of the Association of Her Majesty's District Judges, of 3 St Paul's Square, MK40 1SQ: White man, let me tell you, you are rich ONLY because for several continuous centuries, your white ancestors were THIEVES and owners of stolen children of defenceless poor people, and the African descendants of the robbed do not, yet, have overwhelming power, necessary to demand and extract equitable reparation, and enforce the settlement of several centuries of unpaid accruing interest.

OYINBO OLE: A straight-faced descendant of THIEVES and owners of stolen children of defenceless Africans, including the African ancestors of the great grandchildren of Prince Phillip (1921–2021).

Philippian 1:21: Was Phillip a Mason.

When it inevitably becomes mandatory for Judges to handwrite detailed legal and factual reasons for their decisions, functional semi-illiterate scatter-head closeted white supremacist Antichrist Freemason Judges will be found out.

Then, there, Judges, nearly all, were members of the Antichrist Racist Freemasonry Quasi-Religion (Mediocre Mafia, New Pharisees, New Good Samaritans, Defenders of Faiths, including all the exotic faiths and/or religions associated with the 15 Holy Books in the House of Commons—John 14:6), and some of them were THICKER than a gross of planks—Habakkuk 1:4.

Antichrist Racist Freemasonry Quasi-Religion (Mediocre Mafia, New Pharisees, New Good Samaritans, Defenders of Faiths, including all the exotic faiths and/or religions associated with the 15 Holy Books in the House of Commons—John 14:6) teaches its members secret voodoo handshakes, not grammar, the former is considerably easier to master.

The pattern hereditary racial hatred and incompetent racist lies is the same almost everywhere.

If you disagree with the Antichrist Racist Freemasons (Mediocre Mafia, New Pharisees, New Good Samaritans, Defenders of Faiths, including all the exotic faiths and/or religions associated with the 15 Holy Books in the House of Commons—John 14:6), especially if you are a mere Negro, the closeted racist bastards will kill you, albeit hands-off.

Google: Dr Richard Bamgboye, GP.

Google: Dr Anand Kamath, Dentist.

They were overwhelmed with racist lies, and their minds were tampered with, and they were mercilessly killed, albeit hands-off.

They came to Great Britain for better-life, and closeted hereditary white supremacist bastards prematurely, forcibly, sent them to afterlife. Their hands-off racist killers are not immortal, so they must go to them, as they will never return to them—2 Samuel 12:23.

They hate us, with merciless racist passion, more than their ancestors hated ours, and we know, and they persecute our people (Africans) for the dark coat that we neither made nor chose, and vindictive and extremely ruthless racist bastards, maliciously impede the ascent of our people (Africans) from the bottomless crater into which their insatiably greedy and racist ancestors threw ours—during several centuries of merciless racist evil: The greediest economic cannibalism and the evilest racist terrorism the world will ever know—Habakkuk 2:5.

They should rewrite their law: 'Freedom of expression for adults with the basic skills of a child (imbeciles)' should replace 'Freedom of Expression for all'.

Unlike her little brother, age saved the child's sister from the Closeted-Racist-Dylan–Roof-Freemason-Judge. She thanks her stars that the incontrovertibly functional semi-illiterate, closeted racist white man did not have anything to do with her education.

In her GCSE, she gained the following grades:

English Language A*,

English Literature A*,

Mathematics A*,

Additional Mathematics A*,

Physics A*,

Chemistry A*,

Biology A*,

History A*,

Latin A,

Spanish A,

Advanced Level Mathematics A.

Envy is a thief.

Indiscreet envy.

"Envy is weak." Yul Brynner.

Their centuries-old unspoken myth that intellect is related to their universally acknowledged irrefutably superior skin colour that the very, very, fortunate wearer neither made nor chose—is the mother of all racist scams.

Education, formal and informal, will polish only what genetic mixes present to it, and there is considerably more to genetic mix than skin colour.

The academic height that the white father and mother of the closeted hereditary racist white Bedford's District Judge CANNOT know, and which the natural talents of his own white children will not exploit.

Perception is grander than reality.

White Privilege: They hate us, and we know.

What they want for their own white children is very, very, different from what they want for our own black children, and what they want for their own white children is what we want for our own black children.

"All men are created equal." Abraham Lincoln.

A liar.

"To the American founding fathers, the 'truth that all men are created equal' was 'self-evident'. It'd better be, for it certainly can't be proved. True equality can only exist in heaven; on earth, the belief that all men are created equal is wishful thinking. For men are created unequal in strength, intelligence, character—well, in everything. Earthly inequality is thus a natural order of things, and it can only be distorted by unnatural means. Even then it won't disappear; it'll be replaced by a worse type of inequality or else camouflaged by demagoguery." Alexander Boot, 2011.

If all the White Master Builders (33rd Degree Freemasons—Scottish Rite), they're all white, at the Bedfordshire Masonic Temple, the keep, Bedford Rd, Kempston, Bedford MK42 8AH, could disprove the truth that all the white children of the Senior Vice President of the Association of Her Majesty's District Judges, as implied by OECD, were, most probably, inferiorly created by Almighty God, certainly, intellectually, it should confirm the belief of billions of people, which is that Antichrist Freemasonry Quasi-Religion, Antichrist Islam, Antichrist Judaism, and all other motley assemblies of exotic religions and faiths under the Common Umbrella of the Governor of the Church of England and the Defender of the FAITH—are not intellectually flawed Satanic Mumbo Jumbo, and it will also confirm that reasoning and vision have boundaries, and if reasoning and vision are finite boundaries, He must have lied when, before the Council, He disclosed pictures that His unbounded mind painted, and He must have also lied, when He audaciously stated: "I am the way and the truth and the life. No one comes to the Father except through me" (John 14:6). If the fellow told the truth before the Council, everything that is not aligned to John 14:6 is traveling in the wrong direction and heading straight for very hard rocks.

The brain isn't skin colour; then, we were robbed with guns.

The child sister has since gained a First-Class Science Degree from one of the topmost Universities in the UK, and she's gainfully engaged, batting for her Country.

The Negro is a patriot.

Christ saved the child's sister from the evil clutches of the Closeted Racist Freemason Thugs (Mediocre Mafia, New Pharisees, New Good Samaritans, Defenders of Faiths, including all the exotic faiths and/or religions associated with the 15 Holy Books in the House of Commons—John 14:6) —Habakkuk 1:4.

It's plainly deductible that all the white children of the white Senior Vice President of the Association of Her Majesty's District Judges, were inferiorly created by Almighty God, certainly intellectually—OECD.

https://www.youtube.com/watch?v=BlpH4hG7m1A.

If one were to ask the incontrovertibly functional semi-illiterate white man, albeit England's Class Senior Judge, to bring out his own white children, and if he agrees, and if one were to ask his white children to handwrite a short essay, and if they agreed, and if they could write legibly, Dr Richard Dawkins and OECD implied that they should be duller than their white father, a former debt collector Solicitor in Norwich and a High Ranking Functional Semi-illiterate Freemason (Scottish-Rite).

Facts are sacred, and they cannot be overstated.

"The truth allows no choice." Dr Samuel Johnson.

Based on available evidence, genetic damage is the most enduring residue of several centuries of European Christians' sadistic commerce in millions of stolen children of defenceless poor people (Kamala's ancestors)—Habakkuk.

Then, white privileged dullards were more familiar with Africans of Caribbean extraction: Direct descendants of stolen, carried, and sold Africans: Captured, stolen, sold Africans who were unnaturally selected, genetically reversed, artificially bred for very hard labour, and reared like cattle on stolen plantations, in stolen the New World, by very, very, highly civilised, super enlightened, and ultra-righteous white European Christians – Habakkuk.

OYINBO OLE: Ignorant racist bastards. Ultra-righteous descendants of THIEVES and owners of stolen children of other people– Habakkuk.

Percentage of children in the UK hitting educational targets at 5, in descending order:

1. Asian (Indian).

2. Asian (Any other Asian).

3. White (British).

4. White (Irish).

5. Mixed (any other).

6. Mixed (white and black African).

7. Chinese.

8. Mixed (White and black Caribbean).

9. Black (African heritage).

10. Asian (Any other Asian).

11. Black (Caribbean heritage).

12. Black (other).

13. Asian (Bangladeshi).

14. White (Any other white).

15. Any other ethnic group.

16. Asian (Pakistani).

17. White (Traveller of Irish heritage).

18. White (Gypsy/ Roma).

Source: Centre Forum, 2016.

Children in the UK hitting educational targets at 16, in descending order:

1. Chinese.

2. Asian (Indian).

3. Asian (Any other Asian).

4. Mixed (White and Asian).

5. White (Irish).

6. Mixed (Any other).

7. Any other ethnic group.

8. Asian (Bangladeshi).

9. Parent/pupil preferred not to say.

10. Mixed (White and black African).

11. White (Any other white).

12. Black (African heritage).

13. White (British).

14. Asian (Pakistani).

15. Black (other).

16. Mixed (White and black Caribbean).

17. Black (Caribbean heritage).

18. White (Traveller of Irish heritage).

19. White (Gypsy/ Roma).

Source: Centre Forum, 2016.

Then, on stolen plantations in stolen New Worlds where stolen African children were incarcerated, and compelled to pick cotton and cut cane, at gunpoint, the brightest among to the stolen African children rebelled against indefinite servitude, and they were unnaturally deselected, and the removal of the brightest African genes weakened the common genetic pool of the enslaved Africans. Of the rest, the placid ones refused to voluntary make slave babies, not only because they hated their wicked racist owners, as they did not want to make them richer—the owner of the cow owned its calves, they refused to voluntary make slave babies because it would have been extremely selfish and brainless to wilfully impose indefinite servitude of innocent children, but very, very, many were raped, including paedophilic rape, by very, very, highly civilised and super enlightened sex-machine white European Christians, their owners, and they involuntarily made slave babies and made their owners considerably richer. The armed, white, and civilised European Christians selected the most beautiful boys and girls for their personal sexual enjoyment (House Negroes), and the sensuous, enslaved Africa girls became Mulatto Slave Babies' Factory.

"The white man is the devil." Elijah Mohammed (1897 – 1975).

Based on cogent, irrefutable, and available evidence, the white man isn't only the devil, he is also a THIEF – Habakkuk.

The rest of the stolen Africans were unnaturally paired up, artificially bred for labour, and reared like cattle on stolen plantations in the stolen New World.

Oyinbo ole: Ignorant descendants of thieves and owners of stolen human beings—Habakkuk.

They are psychologically and intellectually insecure, and they hate us with merciless racist passion, and they will bend and break their laws to destroy us, and we know – Habakkuk 1:4.

According to Centre Forum, in 2016, Yellow children (Chinese) were the 1st on the list of those meeting academic targets at age 16.

If yellow people (Chinese) were allowed a free choice, they wouldn't allow members of the White British Ethnic Group who were 13th on the list of those meeting academic targets at age 16, to guide the education of their yellow children,

 So, why should Nigerians (Africans) who were above the white British Group on the list of those meeting academic targets, at age 16—allow a White Gypsy District Judge, a mere former debt-collector Solicitor in Norwich, albeit a former 5th Rate Partner, with arbitrarily acquired camouflage English names, whose ethnic group, White

(Gypsy/ Roma), were last on the list of children meeting academic targets at age 16, to have a say in the education o an African child?

They need intellectual superiority, but he doesn't like them, so He gave them the universally acknowledged irrefutably superior skin colour, and in protest, closeted hereditary white supremacist bastards criminally stole what He gave to AFRICANS.

Bedford, England: GDC, Freemason, Brother, Richard William Hill (NHS Postgraduate Tutor), unrelentingly lied under oath—Habakkuk 1:4.

A very, very, dishonest white man.

A racist crooked Freemason.

Had verifiably crooked, and closeted hereditary white supremacist, Freemason, Brother, Richard William Hill (NHS Postgraduate Tutor), been black, or had the Judges been black, he would have been in trouble – Habakkuk 1:4.

Facts are sacred, and they cannot be overstated.

Then, yields of millions of stolen African children were used to build very, very, Grand Cathedral Courts, and they paid the salaries of white Judges who sent white people who stole money to prisons built with yields of stolen black lives.

Bedford's District Judge Paul Robert Ayers, 70, a Mason, and the Senior Vice President of the Association of Her Majesty's District Judges, of 3 St Paul's Square, MK40 1SQ, which part of our Grand Cathedral County Court, 3,

St Paul's Square, MK40 1SQ, is the yield of your implied extraordinary talent, or which part of it is the yield of the Higher IQ of your own white mother and father, or which part of it did the very, very, good people of Bedford buy, or which part of it did transparent virtue yield, or which part of it preceded SLAVERY: The building or its chattels - Habakkuk?

OYINBO OMO OLE: An ignorant straight-faced descendant of ultra-righteous white thieves and owners of stolen poor black children of defenceless Africans, including the African ancestors of Meghan Markle's white children - Habakkuk.

If we aren't very, very, smart, why are we very, very, rich?

Shepherds didn't bring stolen African children home, and they deceived their own mentally gentler white children that they were paragons of wisdom and virtue who, like Mother Teresa of Calcutta, did only virtuous works in Africa.

CHAPTER SEVEN: Apartheid by stealth. An African whistle blower.

If there is cogent and irrefutable evidence that the white ancestors of one's white mother and father were THIEVES and owners of stolen poor black children of defenceless Africans, including the African ancestors of Meghan Markle's white children, it will be very, very, naive not to expect RACIAL HATRED complicated by incompetent mendacity to be part of one's genetic inheritances, as we are all who we are, the genes of our individual ancestors. Then, their legal system was equal for blacks and whites, but the administration of their bastardised, unashamedly mediocre, indiscreetly dishonest, potently weaponised, vindictive, and institutionally racist system — was not, and the administration of all laws is 'meat', and it is tyrants' tool.

Based on several decades of very, very, proximate observations and direct experiences, and cogent and irrefutable evidence, skin colour that they neither made nor chose is universally acknowledged to be irrefutably superior, but their intellects aren't, and their indiscreetly institutionally racist legal system is fundamentally designed to conceal that truth.

Increasingly universally acknowledged exceptional genetic Nigerians, let me tell you, the fellow is who He says He is – John 14:6, and He is absolutely unplayable:

Ewu nbe loko Alonge. Alonge paapa ewu ni.

Ina njo, ogiri ko sa: Ekan ni omo okunri nku.

Ifura ni oogun awon agbalagba; ifura paapa, agbalagba oogun ni.

MATTHEW 14: John was jailed only because he spoke, and the intolerant lunatic Jew, King Herod, removed his head solely to, permanently, prevent him from speaking.

Is Helen Falcon, MBE, a Jew?

Google: Helen Falcon, Racist Empress.

GDC: Poly-educated Jonathan Martin: Not Russell Group Inferior Education — Proverbs 17:16.

A Racist Crooked White Briton.

Had the indiscreetly crooked hereditary closeted white supremacist bastard, Freemason, Brother, Richard William Hill (NHS Postgraduate Tutor) been black, or had the Judges been black, he would have been in trouble.

Might Judge Constance Briscoe ('ugly' former Judge) have 'WALKED' if she had been Caucasian, English, male, and Freemason?

Then, they were all white, they an informal access to very, very, powerful Freemason Judges.

Scotland, England: GDC, Kevin Atkinson (Scottish Kev), Postgraduate Tutor, Oxford, unrelentingly lied under oath – Habakkuk 1:4.

A very, very, dishonest white man.

A racist descendant of ultra-righteous white thieves and owners of stolen poor black African children of defenceless Africans, including the African ancestors of the white great grandchildren of Prince Phillip (1921 – 2021).

It is plainly deductible that the white Scottish ancestors of the white Scottish mother and father of white Scottish Kevin Atkinson, Postgraduate Tutor, Oxford, were THIEVES: Extremely nasty, vicious, and insatiably greedy merciless racist murders, and owners of stolen poor black children of defenceless Africans, including the African ancestors of Meghan Markle's white children – Habakkuk.

"Time for Scots to say sorry for slavery.

Herald Scotland: Ian Bell, Columnist / Sunday 28 April
2013 / Opinion. According to the American founding
father, the son of a Caithness Kirk's Minister had about
him "an air of great simplicity and honesty'". The likes of
James Boswell and Laurence Sterne also enjoyed the
merchant's company.To his contemporaries, he was, as the
author Adam Hochschild has written, '"a wise, thoughtful
man who embodied the Scottish virtues of frugality,
sobriety, and hard work'". Oswald was a scholar of
theology, philosophy, and history. He collected art,
particularly Rubens and Rembrandt, and gave handsomely
to charity. Oswald, who learned his trade in Glasgow, also
represented Britain in negotiations with the Americans
after their war of liberation. He was the cosmopolitan
epitome of Enlightenment success. But when he wasn't
busy with good works, Oswald waded in blood. The
precise number of deaths that can be laid at his door is
impossible to calculate. As the leading figure in Grant,
Oswald & Co, he had investments in each corner of the
"'triangular trade'". In his own name, Oswald trafficked at
least 13,000 Africans, although he never set foot on their
continent. By the time he bought Auchincruive House and
100,000 acres in Ayrshire in 1764, he was worth £500,000.
Writing in 2005, Hochschild thought this was "'"roughly
equivalent"'" to $68 million (about £44m). This is
conservative. Oswald was remarkable, but not unique.
Where Glasgow and its merchants in sugar, tobacco, and
human life are concerned, there are plenty of names and no
shortage of monuments: Dennistoun, Campbell, Glassford,
Cochrane, Buchanan, Hamilton, Bogle, Ewing, Donald,
Speirs, Dunlop. One way to understand what they wrought
is simple: take pleasure in the city's architecture today and
you are likely to be admiring the fruits of slavery.
Glasgow is not alone in that. London, Liverpool and
Bristol also have their stories to tell. Edinburgh's once-
great banks grew from foundations built on bones. The first

Scottish venture into slavery set out from the capital in 1695. Montrose, Dumfries, Greenock, and Port Glasgow each tried their hands. In the language of the present age, they were all in it together. When commerce was coursing around the triangle, most of polite Scotland was implicated. The nobility (and country) rendered bankrupt in 1700 in the aftermath of the Darien Venture was by the mid-1760s contemplating big, elegant townhouses and 100,000-acre estates. You could call that a reversal of fortune. Contrary to self-serving myth, it did not happen because of "'frugality, sobriety, and hard work". Certain things need to be remembered about Scotland and slavery. One is that the mercantile class got stinking rich twice over: despite fortunes made from stolen lives, they were quick to demand compensation when slavery was ended in 1833. Britain's government decided that £20m, a staggering sum, could be raised. In his 2010 book, The Price of Emancipation, Nicholas Draper reckons Glasgow's mob got £400,000 – in modern terms, hundreds of millions. Compensation cases also demonstrated that Scots were not merely following an English lead. According to Draper, a country with 10% of the British population accounted for at least 15% of absentee slavers. By another estimate, 30% of Jamaican plantations were run by Scots. For all the pride taken in the abolitionist societies of Glasgow and Edinburgh, the slaveholders did not suffer because of abolition. They were '"compensated'".

And that wasn't the worst of it. Thanks to Hollywood movies, the slave economy of the American South is still taken as barbarism's benchmark. Few realise that the behaviour of Scots busy getting rich in the slaveholders" empire was actually worse – routinely worse – than the worst of the cottonocracy. You need only count the corpses................."

Properly rehearsed ultra-righteousness and deceptively
schooled civilised decorum – were preceded by several
continuous centuries of merciless racist evil: The greediest
economic cannibalism and the evilest racist terrorism the
world will ever know – Habakkuk.

They hate us, and we know.

Then, they were a properly organised gang of hereditary
closeted white supremacist criminalised bastards, and when
discerning Nigerians could see them, and they knew that
discerning Nigerians could see them, discerning Nigerians
inadvertently reached the end of their life, as all loose ends
were tied using all means necessary, and they had unbounded
and unaccountable extra-judicial power.

They are racist killers, albeit hands-off.

Google: Dr Richard Bamgboye, GP.

Our own Nigerian and Nigerien babies with huge oil wells,
gas fields, and uranium mines near their huts eat only
1.5/day, a very, very, bellyful, overfed, hereditary closeted
white supremacist bastard, Freemason, Brother, Richard
William Hill (NHS Postgraduate Tutor), whose white mother
and father have never seen crude oil, and whose children
mightn't be able to spell the word 'uranium', and whose
white ancestors were fed like battery hens with yields of

stolen poor black children of defenceless Africans, including the African ancestors of Meghan Markle's white children, thrives in Great Britain, what's great about that?

Google: Mediocre Great England.

President Biden and President Zelensky want Ukrainians to be part our very, very, highly civilised and super-enlightened Free World where white people, only white people, are allowed to fabricate reports and unrelentingly tell incompetent racist lies under oath, and President Putin does not, so he converted Bakhmut from bricks to rubble.

"The Bakhmut of our hearts." President Zelensky.

The Africa of our Hearts: Then, our people used similar words during European Christians' extortionately profitable commerce in millions of stolen poor black African children, including the African ancestors of Meghan Markle's white children – Habakkuk:

Odi arinako, otun wa di oju ala.

Facts are sacred.

"The truth allows no choice." Dr Samuel Johnson

It is a very, very, grand deceit that Nigerians are equal under the English Law.

Only historical imbeciles, myopic fantasists, delusional idealists, utopians, and generally excessively stupid Nigerians expect closeted hereditary white supremacist Freemason Judges to measure their own people with the same yardstick they use to measure our own people (African Bombatas)

CHAPTER EIGHT: Dr Ngozi Ekweremadu.

An ignorant racist white bastard approved and immortalised what his poly-educated white supervisors in LUTON authorised.

 HHJ Perusko studied Law at Poly, not Russell Group alternative education – Proverbs 17:16.

"The best opportunity of developing academically and emotional." Bedford's District Judge Paul Robert Ayers, 70, a Mason, and the Senior Vice President of the Association of Her Majesty's District Judges, of 3 St Paul's Square, MK40 1SQ.

A closeted hereditary racist descendant of ultra-righteous white THIEVES and owners of stolen human beings, including poor black children of defenceless Africans, including the African ancestors of Meghan Markle's white children—Habakkuk.

An ultra-righteous descendant of extremely nasty, vicious, and merciless racist murderers, industrial-scale professional armed robbers and armed land grabbers, gun runners, opium merchants (drug dealers), and owners of millions of stolen poor black children of defenceless Africans, including the African ancestors of Meghan Markle's white children – Habakkuk.

"I know of no evil that has ever existed, nor can imagine any evil to exist, worse than the tearing of eighty thousand persons annually from their native land, by a combination of the most civilised nations inhabiting the most enlightened part of the globe, but more especially under the sanction of the laws of that Nation which calls herself the most free and the most happy of them all." Prime Minister William Pitt the Younger

OYINBO OLE Based on several decades of very, very, proximate observations and direct experiences, they are obsessed with money, other people's money.

Bedford's District Judge Paul Robert Ayers, > 70, a Mason, and the Senior Vice President of Her Majesty District Judges, 3, St Paul's Square, MK40 1SQ: Based on cogent, irrefutable, and available evidence, it is the absolute truth that the white ancestors of your white mother and father were THIEVES and owners of stolen poor black children of defenceless Africans, including the African ancestors of Meghan Markle's white children – Habakkuk.

"Many Scots masters were considered among the most brutal, with life expectancy on their plantations averaging a mere four years. We worked them to death then simply imported more to keep the sugar and thus the money flowing. Unlike centuries of grief and murder, an apology cost nothing. So, what does Scotland have to say?" Herald Scotland: Ian Bell, Columnist, Sunday 28 April 2013

Based on several decades of very, very, proximate observations and direct experiences, they are obsessed with money, stolen money.

"There are few more impressive sights in the world than a Scotsman on the make." Sir James M. Barrie

SCOTLAND, ENGLAND: GDC, Kevin Atkinson, Dentist, our Postgraduate Tutor, Oxford, unrelentingly lied under oath – Habakkuk I:4.

A very, very, dishonest Scottish crook.

A racist descendant of Scottish THIEVES and owners of poor black stolen children of defenceless Africans, including the African ancestors of the niece and nephew of the Prince of Wales.

Based on several decades of very, very, proximate observations and direct experiences, Scotsmen are grossly overrated: Perception is grander that reality.

Nigerien babies with gigantic uranium mines near their huts eat only1.5/day in our own West Africa, a very, very, bellyful overfed scatter-head Scotsman, a closeted hereditary closeted white supremacist bastard who white mother and father mightn't know the meaning of uranium, and whose children mightn't be able to spell uranium,

"As hard hearted as the Scot of Scotland." English saying

"Gie a Scotsman an inch, and he'll take an 'ell." Scottish saying

If all the very, very charitable closeted hereditary white supremacist Freemasons in Edinburgh and Glasgow (Scottish Rite): Masonic Centre, 101 Clifford Street, Glasgow, G51 1QP, and Freemasons Hall, 96 George St, Edinburgh EH2 3DH, could disprove the truth that GDC, Kevin Atkinson, Dentist, our Postgraduate Tutor, Oxford, unrelentingly lied under oath – Habakkuk I:4, they will confirm the belief of millions of Scots Scotland that which is that Charitable Antichrist Freemasonry Quasi-Religion (Mediocre Mafia, New Pharisees, New Good Samaritans, Defenders of Faiths, including all the Faiths and/or Religions associated with the 15 Holy Books in the House of Commons, and Dissenters of the Faith — John 14:6), Antichrist Islam, Antichrist Judaism, and all other motley assemblies of Religions and Faiths under the Common Umbrella of the Governor of the Church of England, and the Defender of the Faith — John 14:6, are not intellectually flawed Satanic Mumbo Jumbo, and they will also confirm that reasoning and vision have finite boundaries, and if reasoning and vision have finite boundaries, the fellow must have been dishonest, before the Council, when He purportedly disclosed pictures His infinite mind painted, and He must have lied when He audaciously declared that He is extra-terrestrial, exceptional, and immortal — John 14:6.

If the fellow told Jews and Romans the truth in the Council, we are FORKED, all of us, as His Knights attack all Kings and Queens simultaneously, and only the Queens can move, and everything, absolutely everything that is not aligned with His Divine Exceptionalism (John 5:22, John 14:6) is travelling in the wrong direction and heading straight for the ROCKS.

It does no harm to throw the occasional man overboard, but it does not do much good if you are steering full speed ahead for the rocks." Sir Ian Gilmour (1926–2007).

Facts are sacred, and they cannot be overstated.

MONSTERS: White Privilege and White Supremacy are con-joined twins, with two heads, one fertility, and four left legs, so they move like drunken lunatics.

They are not the only creation of Almighty God, and they are not immortal, and the universally acknowledged irrefutably superior skin colour that the closeted hereditary white supremacist bastards neither made nor chose and God Almighty are truly good (Mark 10:18), but the invaluable asset is not the only wonder of our world.

This, and only this, is the truth. Properly rehearsed ultra-righteousness and deceptively schooled civilised decorum were preceded by several continuous centuries of crude and cruel inhumanity, incapacity to visualise the feelings and sufferings of their African victims, and all driven by insatiable greed.

Habakkuk 25: This, and only this, is the truth. Then, racist white bastards were greedier than the grave, and like death, they were never satisfied, and very, very, highly civilised, super-enlightened, and ultra-righteous European Christians were not deterred by His justice because they did not believe in His exceptionalism _ John 5:22, John 14:6.

Facts are sacred.

"The truth allows no choice." Dr Samuel Johnson

Skin colour is a great creation of Almighty God, but it is not the greatest.

White Supremacy thrives on the subjugation of the truth, which is that the centuries-old unspoken myth that their universally acknowledged irrefutably superior skin colour is related to intellect - is the mother of all racist scams — Habakkuk.

When it became apparent that the fellow with the infinite mind was intellectually unplayable, intolerant bastards lynched Him like Gadhafi and crucified Him, and He was not punished for speaking, He was killed solely to prevent Him from speaking – Matthew 27: 34 – 35.

Habakkuk 2:5: Then, they were greedier than the grave, and like death, they were never satisfied, and by hook or by crook, they always won in Courts, but in the war, when the Corporal flipped, the real Judge looked away, and they lost everything, and more – John 5:22, Matthew 25:31- 46.

https://www.youtube.com/watch?v=BlpH4hG7m1A

"Jews are very good with money." President Trump

The President should know: Bianca and Jared Kushner are Jews.

Based on available evidence, Judas Iscariot (3BC – 30 AD) was a Jew, but he wasn't a Mason. Phillip wasn't a Jew, but was Phillip a 33rd Degree Freemason (Scottish Rite) – Philippian 1:21?

Ghislaine Maxwell's dad, Ján Ludvík Hyman Binyamin Hoch (1923 – 1991), and Bernard Madoff (1938 – 2021) were Jews, and crooks.

It is not the truth that all Jews are crooks.

The real name of Ghislaine Maxwell's dad was Ján Ludvík Hyman Binyamin Hoch (1923 – 1991), and the crooked Jew came from Czechoslovakia in the 40s.

Based on available evidence, GIGANTIC yields of millions of stolen African children (Black Holocaust), not feudal agriculture, lured Eastern European Jews to Great Britain.

Descendants of the victims of NAZI Holocaust are among the principal beneficiaries of the Real Holocaust (Slavery).

The human tragedy during several centuries of merciless racist evil (the greediest economic cannibalism and the evilest racist terrorism the world will ever know) was the real Holocaust, and the tragedy of 1939 – 1945 was a storm in a teacup in comparison.

1807 Act: Africans who believe that they are no longer inferior to white people under English Law should seek redress within it when they are aggrieved, and Africans who know that they, like their ancestors, remain inferior to white people, especially under their law, should turn the other cheek, and avoid their Negrophobic charade, where Negrophobic Perjury guards Persecutory Negrophobia.

There is another Justice – John 5:22, Habakkuk.

A brainless racist white bastard sat on a very, very, highchair that the people of Bedford couldn't and didn't buy, in a Cathedral Court that was preceded by SLAVERY, future flats.

29, Goldington Road is a block of flats.

Then, yields of stolen lives (slavery) were used to build Grand Cathedral Courts, and pay the wages of white Judges who sent white people who stole money to magnificent prisons built with yields of stolen lives (stolen money) — Habakkuk.

Then, they were psychologically and intellectually insecure, and like lunatic Jihadists, Kim, MBS, and babies, they expected all Nigerians to love them unconditionally, and they expected all our people to see our world only from their perspective (Negrophobic unipolarity), and they expected all NIGERIANS to say and/or write only what they love to hear, and any Nigerian with any religious belief not aligned with theirs (faiths) — was undermined and destroyed by intolerant closeted hereditary white supremacist bastards, and dissenters of the faith — John 14:6.

Then, like the teachers of law (Pharisees), for the legal system of Stonemasons (Builders) to work as it was designed, they must be superior, and they were, but only skin colour that they neither made nor chose — was universally acknowledged to be irrefutably superior, their intellect wasn't, and closeted hereditary racist bastards criminally, constructively, cancelled the education of Africans, and they stole yields of Africans' Christ granted talents.

They were hereditary THIEVES - Habakkuk.

CHAPTER NINE: Apartheid by stealth. An African whistleblower.

If there is irrefutable evidence that the white ancestors of one's white mother and father were THIEVES and owners of stolen children of defenceless Africans, including the African ancestors of Meghan Markle's white children, it will be very, very, naive not to expect racial hatred complicated by incompetent mendacity to be part of one's genetic inheritances.

Some very, very, highly civilised and ultra-righteous white people believe that all NIGERIANS were criminals, and they deserved to be subjected to racist criminality, the treatment of choice for Nigerian racist criminals.

Accurate White Seers: They foresaw that a white Welsh imbecile will be our postgraduate tutor, Oxford, they used guns to loot and pillage AFRICA.

"They may not have been well written from a grammatical point of view." Geraint Evans, Postgraduate Tutor, Oxford, of Rowtree Dental Care

A crooked racist white Welshman

NORTHAMPTON, ENGLAND: NHS Postgraduate Tutor, Oxford, Geraint Evans, unrelentingly lied on record. The white Welsh ancestors of his white mother and father were incompetent racist liars too, they were THIEVES and owners of stolen poor black children of defenceless AFRICANS, including the African ancestors of the white niece and nephew of the Prince of Wales.

Facts are sacred, and they cannot be overstated.,

https://www.youtube.com/watch?v=BlpH4hG7m1A

One dimensionally educated historical imbeciles, ignorant descendants of extremely nasty, vicious, and merciless racist murderers, industrial-scale professional armed robbers, gun runners, drug dealers (opium merchants), and owners of millions of stolen poor black children of defenceless Africans, including the African ancestors of Meghan Markle's white children — Habakkuk.

The stone that the builders rejected is now the cornerstone —
Psalm 118:22, Luke 20:17.

"Study history, study history, in history lies all the secrets of
statecraft." Sir Winston Churchill (1874 – 1965)

Based on several decades of very, very, proximate
observations, direct experiences, cogent and irrefutable
evidence, the equality of descendants of slaves and
descendants of owners of stolen children of defenceless
Africans – is an unrealistic aspiration.

Only our visible chains are off; our true chains will never be
voluntarily removed. We are powerless, and we have been
robbed to penniless since theirs found ours in the African
bush in the 15th.

"But no advance in wealth, no softening of manners, no
reform or revolution has ever brought human equality a
millimetre nearer. From the point of view of the Low, no
historic change has ever meant much more than a change in
the name of their masters." George Orwell

White Supremacy is immortal. Why should white people
vacate centuries-old stolen advantageous positions in
exchange for NOTHING?

OYINBO OLE: Only stupid Nigerians, Nigeriens, and other
Africans, myopic fantasists, deluded idealists, utopians, and
historical imbeciles expect white people to voluntarily
relinquish several centuries-old advantageous positions in

exchange for NOTHING, and only stupider Nigerians, Nigeriens, and other Africans expect closeted hereditary white supremacist Freemason Judges to measure white people, their own kindred, with the same yardstick they use to measure Negroes (blacks), and only the stupidest among Negroes (blacks) expect white demons to cast out white demons — Matthew 12:27.

"Change occurs slowly. Very often a legal change might take place, but the cultural shift required to really accept its spirit lingers in the wings for decades." Sara Sheridan.

Like his mentally gentler white children, the white imbeciles (predominantly but not exclusively white adults with the basic skills of a child) who sat before him did not know that his nomination and constructive appointment as our District Judge by some dementing and/or demented white Lords— was not based on progressive, measurable, and colour-blind objectivity, and they did not know that the last time the closeted hereditary white supremacist bastard passed through the filter of objectivity was when he studied 5th rate law at Poly, and it showed.

Then, Alzheimer's disease was not uncommon in the House of Lords, and it was considerably more common than ordinarily realised, and it was incompatible with the competent administration of English Law, and the competent administration of English Law should be an inviolable basic right.

"This man I thought had been a Lord of wits, but I find he's only a wit among Lords." Dr Samuel Johnson.

Dr Samuel Johnson implied that in his era, Lords were relatively dull.

"Should 500 men, ordinary men, chosen accidentally from among the unemployed, override the judgement — the deliberate judgement — of millions of people who are engaged in the industry which makes the wealth of the country?" David Lloyd George (1863–1945).

BEDFORD, ENGLAND: District Judge **Paul Robert Ayers, > 70, a Mason, and the Senior Vice President of Her Majesty District Judges, 3, St Paul's Square, MK40 1SQ,** based on available evidence, the white ancestors of your own white mother and father were THIEVES and owners of stolen poor black West African children, our own direct ancestors, including the ancestors of Meghan Markle's white children.

Facts are sacred.

"The truth allows no choice." Dr Samuel Johnson.

White man, let me tell you, white man, you are worthy only because you're white and England is very rich, apart from those, you are PURIFIED NOTHING.

It is plainly deductible that your Christ granted talent and yields of the land on which your own white mother and father were born cannot sustain your very, very, high standard of living. You are a THIEF, but only by heritage, and because equitable reparation pends, and several centuries of unpaid interest accrue. When we inevitably acquire nukes, closeted hereditary white supremacist bastards will be forced to shit out every penny owed — Habakkuk.

2 Thessalonians 3: 6–10: Which one of our putrid tubes did our Born-Again Christian tell our Bedford Mason District Judge Judge Paul Robert Ayers, > 70, a Mason, and the Senior Vice President of Her Majesty District Judges, 3, St Paul's Square, MK40 1SQ and Masons at Brickhill Baptist Church, Bedford—she used to work for £0.5M?

BEDFORD, ENGLAND: District Judge Paul Robert Ayers, > 70, a Mason, and the Senior Vice President of Her Majesty District Judges, 3, St Paul's Square, MK40 1SQ, based on available evidence, our own money, NIGERIA (oil/gas), is by far more relevant to the economic survival of your white spouse, your white mother, your white father, and all your white children than the Northampton of Northants' patriots (BNP).

Based on available evidence, it is absolutely impossible for your talent and yields of the land on which your own white mother and father were born to sustain your high standard of living.

Based on available evidence the white ancestors of your white mother and father were industrial-scale professional thieves and owners of stolen poor black children of defenceless Africans, including the West African ancestors of Meghan Markle's white children - Habakkuk.

They are very, very, highly civilised, and super enlightened, and they do everything, strictly according to the rule of their law, including racial hatred and fraud— Habakkuk 1:4.

There were laws during slavery.

Equitable, and just, reparation pends, and several centuries of unpaid interest accrue.

OYINBO OLE: Then, ignorant descendants of Alphonse Gabriel deceived their own mentally gentler children that they were Archangel Gabriel.

"The may not have been well written from a grammatical point of view ….." Dr Geraint Evans, of Rowtree Dental Care, Rowtree Road, Northampton NN4 0NY, our postgraduate Tutor, Oxford.

Our Welsh imbecile of our Empire of Stolen Affluence— Habakkuk.

A closeted hereditary white supremacist bastard immortalised in writing what his white Welsh father and mother spoke, which Mrs Helen Falcon, MBE, his supervisor, authorised.

Google: Helen Falcon, Racist Empress.

Mrs Helen Falcon, Member of the Most Excellent Order of our Empire reminded one of the ugly Welsh wenches a Scottish poet interacted with.

"The ordinary women of Wales are general short and squat, ill-favoured, and nasty." David Mallet (1705–1765).

President Putin did not want President Zelensky and Ukrainians to be part of our very, very, highly civilised, super-enlightened, and Free World, where a Welsh imbecile could become our Postgraduate Tutor, Oxford, so he used guns to steal Crimea.

Irish Joe, how much cash did your Catholic ancestors have in their pockets when they disembarked in America, in the 19th century, without luggage or decent shoes?

European Christians used guns to dispossess Native Americans and stole their land.

"All have taken what had other owners, and all have had recourse to arms rather than quit the prey onto which they were fastened." Dr Samuel Johnson.

Our own NIGERIA, Shell's docile cash cow since 1956: Our own Nigerian babies with gigantic oil wells and gas fields near their huts eat only 1.5/day in our own NIGERIA, a very, very, bellyful, overfed, and closeted hereditary white supremacist bastard whose white Welsh mother and father have never seen crude, as unlike Putin's

Russia, there are no oil wells or gas fields in Wales, and whose white Welsh ancestors, including the white Welsh ancestors of Aneurin Bevan (1897–1960), were fed like battery hens with yields of stolen poor black children of defenceless Africans, including the African ancestors of the white niece and nephew of the Prince of Wales, is our Postgraduate Tutor, Oxford, Great Britain, what's great about that?

Aneurin Bevan's NHS was preceded by slavery; it paid for it.

OYINBO OLE: An ignorant descendant of very, very, hardened PROFESSIONAL THIEVES and owners of stolen children of other people—Habakkuk.

Based on several decades of very, very, proximate observations and direct experiences, then, they maliciously persecuted our people for the dark coat that we neither made nor chose, and motivated by uncontrollable vindictiveness and hereditary racial hatred, they constructively cancelled the education of self-educated Africans who disagreed with them, and they, criminally, stole yields of our Christ granted talents, and very, very, highly civilised and super enlightened Europeans did everything legally, and strictly according to the rule of their law, and the weapon of the direct descendants of the father of lies (John 8:44) was the mother of all racist lies, and their power was the certainty that all Judges will be white, and their hope was that all Judges will be closeted racist white bastards too.

Homogeneity in the administration of their law is the impregnable secure mask of merciless racist evil.

Based on several decades of very, very, proximate observations and direct experiences, they are psychologically and intellectually insecure, and they are more intolerant to other views than lunatic Jihadists.

They are extremely wicked people: Straight-faced descendants of thieves and owners of stolen poor children of defenceless Africans, including the African ancestors of Meghan Markle's white children.

Negrophobic Perjury guards Persecutory Negrophobia. Before uncontrollable hereditary racial hatred complicated by incompetent mendacity unravels, it is a conspiracy theory, and when it does, it instantly mutates to a mistake.

Then, racist white bastards used gun to steal for white people (Slavery), now, white people use incompetent racist lies to steal for white people – Habakkuk 1:4

NORTHAMPTON, ENGLAND: GDC, Dr Geraint Evans, Postgraduate Tutor, Oxford, of Rowtree Dental Care, Rowtree Road, Northampton NN4 0NY, Northampton, unrelentingly lied under oath (on record)—Habakkuk 1:4.

A very, very, dishonest crooked Welshman. A closeted hereditary white supremacist bastard.

Then, and only there, Africans couldn't defend themselves against crooked racist white bastards before crooked racist white bastards – Habakkuk.

He's white, and his whiteness seemed to be his most valuable asset as a human being.

"The earth contains no race of human beings, so totally vile and worthless as the Welsh …." Walter Savage Landor.

Had he been black or had the Judges been black, he would have been in trouble. Then, theirs was an indiscreetly institutionally racist legal system that was overseen by closeted hereditary white supremacist Freemason Judges — Habakkuk 1:4.

If all the Freemason Judges in Wales, including all the 33rd Degree Freemasons at Cardiff Masonic Hall, 8 Guildford St, Cardiff CF10 2HL, could disprove the truth that GDC, Dr Geraint Evans, Postgraduate Tutor, Oxford, of Rowtree Dental Care, Northampton, unrelentingly lied under oath)on record)—Habakkuk 1:4, they will confirm the belief of millions of Welsh people, which is that Charitable Antichrist Freemasonry Quasi-Religion (Mediocre Mafia, New Pharisees, New Good Samaritans, Defenders of Faiths, including all the Faiths and/or Religions associated with the 15 Holy Books in the House of Commons, and Dissenters of the Faith—John 14:6), Antichrist Islam, Antichrist Judaism, and all other motley assemblies of Religions and Faiths under the Common Umbrella of the Governor of the Church of England, and the Defender of the Faith—John 14:6, are not intellectually flawed Satanic

Mumbo Jumbo, and they will also confirm that reasoning and vision have finite boundaries, and if reasoning and vision have finite boundaries, the fellow must have been dishonest, before the Council, when He purportedly disclosed pictures His infinite mind painted, and He must have lied when He audaciously declared that He is extra-terrestrial, exceptional, and immortal—John 14:6.

If the fellow told Jews and Romans the truth in the Council, we are FORKED, all of us, as His Knights attack all Kings and Queens simultaneously, and only the Queens can move, and everything, absolutely everything that is not aligned with His Divine Exceptionalism (John 5:22, John 14:6) is travelling in the wrong direction and heading straight for the ROCKS.

"It does no harm to throw the occasional man overboard, but it does not do much good if you are steering full speed ahead for the rocks." Sir Ian Gilmour (1926–2007).

Facts are sacred, and they cannot be overstated.

CHAPTER TEN: Dr Ngozi Ekweremadu

BEDFORD, ENGLAND: District Judge Paul Robert Ayers, > 70, a Mason, and the Senior Vice President of Her Majesty District Judges, 3, St Paul's Square, MK40 1SQ, white man, let me tell you, you are worthy only because you're white and England is rich, apart from those, you're purified NOTHING. It's absolutely impossible for your talent and yields of the land on which your white mother and father were born to sustain your higher standard of living. Our own money, Nigeria (oil/gas) is by far more relevant to the economic survival of your white spouse, your white mother, your white father, and all your white children than LUTON. The white ancestors of your mother and mother were ultra-righteous white THIEVES and owners of stolen poor black children of defenceless AFRICANS—Habakkuk.

OYINBO OLE: An ignorant white supremacist bastard. An ultra-righteous descendant of professional armed robbers and owners of stolen human beings, including the African ancestors of Prince Harry's white children—Habakkuk.

BEDFORD, ENGLAND: District Judge Paul Robert Ayers, > 70, a Mason, and the Senior Vice President of Her Majesty District Judges, 3, St Paul's Square, MK40 1SQ, all properly self-educated Nigerian should be very, very, familiar with your history, particularly your economic history, and they should know too many things you don't. Based on available evidence, the white ancestors of your white mother and father were THIEVES and owners of stolen poor black children of defenceless Africans, including the African ancestors of Meghan Markle's white children. Facts are sacred, and they cannot be overstated. Based on cogent and irrefutable evidence, it is possible to use cogent facts and irrefutable evidence to uncover you and the system you serve.

You are FROTH: Only your superior skin colour and Almighty God are truly good — Mark 10:18, and you neither made nor chose it, and you will be considerably diminished as a human being without it, and you know it.

Facts are sacred, and they cannot be overstated.

Their hairs stand on end when they are challenged by Africans.

We and our type are the ones racist bastards will beat up without the support of the YANKS.

With the support of Europeans, but without the support of the YANKS, Ukraine would have surrendered.

The USA is NATO, and everything else is an auxiliary bluff.

OXFORD, ENGLAND: GDC, British Soldier, Stephanie Twidale (TD) unrelentingly lied under oath – Habakkuk 1:4.

A very, very, dishonest white woman.

A crooked closeted hereditary white supremacist British Soldier (Territorial Defence).

The pattern is the same everywhere.

Then, they were all crooked closeted hereditary white supremacist bastards.

They are very, very, angry because we refuse to buy their confidence trickery, as we sincerely do not believe that we are no longer generally considered to be inferior to white people (Apartheid by stealth), and it is dishonesty that after their 1807 Act, we are no longer inferior to white people, under their law, and before white Judges — Habakkuk 1:4.

Then, they carried and sold millions of stolen children from our own West Africa, including the Nigerian ancestors of our Meghan Markle's white children, now, they steal our own natural resources from our own West Africa, including Nigerien uranium.

Substitution is continuing exploitative fraud, not emancipation.

"Moderation is a virtue only among those who are thought to have found alternatives." Henry Kissinger

"The white woman is the devil." Mohammed Ali (1942 - 2016) paraphrased.

Based on cogent and irrefutable evidence, and several continuous decades of very, very, proximate observations and direct experiences, the white woman is not only the devil, but she is also a THIEF.

OYINBO OLE: If there is cogent and irrefutable evidence that the white ancestors of one's white mother and father were THIEVES and owners of stolen poor black children of defenceless Africans, it will be very, very, naïve not to expect RACIAL HATRED complicated by incompetent mendacity to be part of one's genetic inheritances.

Their people are everywhere (Members of the very, very charitable Freemasonry Fraternity), and they control almost everything in Great Britain, especially the administration of their law, and the Antichrist dissenters of the Faith (John 14:6) constructively impose racial hatred and fraud, with integrity, friendship, and respect – John 14:6.

OXFORD, ENGLAND: GDC, Bristol University Educated Mrs Helen Falcon, MBE, Member of the Most Excellent Order of our Empire, a former Member of the GDC Committee, a former Postgraduate Dean, Oxford, a very, very, charitable Rotarian (Quasi-Freemason), and the spouse of Mr Falcon, unrelentingly lied under oath (on record) — Habakkuk 1:4.

A very, very, dishonest white woman.

A closeted hereditary white supremacist Member of the Most Excellent Order of our Empire of Stolen Affluence — Habakkuk.

Helen Falcon Member of the Most Excellent Order of our Empire (MBE), let me tell you, only your skin colour is universally acknowledged to be irrefutably superior, and you neither made nor chose the invaluable asset, and it is absolutely impossible for you to compete on a level intellectual and colour-blind playing field without resorting to racist criminality. An ignorant descendant of THIEVES and owners of stolen children of defenceless poor people (Africans), including the African ancestors of Meghan Markle's white children. A closeted hereditary white supremacist and mere DMF.

BEDFORD, ENGLAND: District Judge Paul Robert Ayers, > 70, a Mason, and the Senior Vice President of Her Majesty District Judges, 3, St Paul's Square, MK40 1SQ, how many stolen African children did yellow people carry and sell?

Before racist crimes of closeted hereditary white supremacist bastards implode and simultaneously explode, they are conspiracy theories, and when they do, they instantly mutate to mistakes.

Then, and only there, when their people committed racist crimes against ours, their people who oversaw the administration of their law (closeted hereditary white supremacist Freemason Judges) criminally buried RACIAL HATRED.

Then, and only there, when closeted hereditary white supremacist criminals knew that you could see them, you have, inadvertently, reached the end of your life as all loose ends must be tied.

ACHROMATOPSIA: Then, closeted hereditary white supremacist bastards could see Nigerians in the dark, but they couldn't see their own white kindred on a very bright sunny day – Matthew VII.

Based on several decades of very, very, proximate observations and direct experiences, not all white people are as indiscreetly racist as Ron Atkinson, but nearly all white people are closeted white supremacists.

CHAPTER ELEVEN: Apartheid by stealth. An African whistleblower.

G DC: Helen Falcon (MBE) lied.

OUR CROOKED RACIST MBE.

"He's what is known in some schools as a fu*king lazy thick nig*er." Ron Atkinson, a former Manchester United Manager. "What I said was racist — but I'm not a racist. I am an idiot." Ron Atkinson, a former Manchester United Manager.

An ignorant closeted hereditary white supremacist bastard, a very, very, brilliant descendant of ultra-righteous PROFESIONAL WHITE THIEVES and owners of stolen black children of defenceless Africans, including the African ancestors of Meghan Markle's white children — Habakkuk.

Then, the white ancestors of Ron Atkinson, and Kevin Atkinson (Scottish Kev) carried and sold millions of stolen poor black children, including the ancestors of fu*king lazy thick nig*ers, and including the African ancestors of the white great grandchildren of Prince Phillip (1921–2021).

Philippian 1:21. Was Phillip a 33rd Degree Mason, Scottish-Rite?

Genetic damage is the most enduring residue of several continuous centuries of merciless racist evil: The greediest economic cannibalism and the evilest racist terrorism the world will ever know (SLAVERY).

Then, closeted hereditary white supremacist bastards were greedier than the grave, and like death, they were never satisfied — Habakkuk 2:5.

Now, greedy racist bastards steal natural resources from West Africa, including Nigerians' oil and gas, and Nigeriens' uranium.

SUBSTITUTION IS FRAUDULENT EMANCIPATION.

"Moderation is a virtue only among those who are thought to have found alternatives." Henry Kissinger.

Then, closeted hereditary white supremacist bastards knew how to steal for their own white kindred, but they didn't know how to repair the scatter — heads of their own white kindred.

"This statement is about a series of letters and emails I have been recieving. I am the above named person. I live at an address provided to police. In this statement I will also mention XXXXXXXXXXXXXXXXXXXXXXXXXXXX a leaseholder for a property I manage at my place work. I am the company director of DOBERN properties based in Ilford. These emails have been sent to my company email address of mail@debern.co.uk, and also letters have been sent to myself at our company ADDress of P.O BOX 1289, ILFORD, IG2 7XZ over the last Two and a half years, I have recieving a series of letters and emails from DR BAMGeLu. DR BAMGBELU is a leasholder for a property I manage at my place of work. Over the period of his leaseholding, DR BAmGelu has continually failed to pay arrears for the property. In march 2016 my company took DR to court and he was ordered to pay outstanding costs of around £20000 since that time and lead up to the case, DR BaMGBelu has been emailing me and posting me letters that are lengthy and accuses me repeatedly of being a racist in emails and letters tact are regularly Ten to twelve pages long, DR BAMGBELU. lists numerous quots from google searches all refrencing ham I am a bigot and a racist. The most recent letter I received from DR BAMGBELU opens with you are jealous and racist Evil combination you hate us we know it" he goes on to say "I would not have knowingly had anything to do with white supremicists." In the last email I recieved from him on 02/09/2016 DR BaMGBELU stated "you are restricted by poor Education within one of the least literate countries in the world". I would be perfectly happy for DR BAMGBElu to contact myself or my company if he has relevant enquiries to his lease holding, however these continuous letters and emails are causing me distress and I feel intimidated. I am not a racist and these accusatios make uncomfortable. All I want is to conduct between us in a normal manner. I want BambGlu to stop emailing me and sending me letters accusing me of being racist and harassing me." MR ROBERT KINGSTON, SOLICITOR, ACCOUNTANT, AND COMPANY DIRECTOR.

A scatter-head white man.

Dyslexia is hereditary but is incompetent mendacity hereditary?

A very special tailless white monkey seemed to have the intellect of black monkeys with tails.

OYINBO OLE: WHITE THIEVES: HABAKKUK.

Based on several decades of very, very, proximate observations and direct experiences, the white man is grossly overrated.

They persecute our people for the dark coat that we neither made nor chose, and cannot change, and they steal the yields of our Christ granted talents, and they maliciously impede our ascent from the bottomless crater into which their very, very, sadistic, and ancestors threw ours, in the African bush, unprovoked, during several continuous centuries of merciless

racist evil: The greediest and the evilest economic
cannibalism, and crudest and cruelest racist terrorism the
world will ever know.

He is watching them — John 5:22.

The nemesis is not extinct, and the fact that it tarries isn't
proof that it will never come — Habakkuk; Proverbs 15:3;
Matthew 25: 31–46. Then, they were greedier than the grave,
and like death, they were never satisfied — Habakkuk 2:5.

Then, very, very, greedy bastards won in courts, but in the
war, when the Corporal flipped, the only true Judge looked
away, and very, very, greedy bastards lost EVERYTHING,
and a lot more.

"Jews are very good with money." President Donald Trump.

Their President should know a thing or two about Jews, and
Bianca and Jared Kushner are Jews.

Everyone knows that Jews are very good with money, and
the Corporal did too, but whose cash are Jews very, very,
good with?

Judas Iscariot, Ghislaine Maxwell's father, Ján Ludvík
Hyman Binyamin Hoch, and Bernard Madoff - were Jews.

President Joe Biden, how come only 1.4% of Americans are Jews, and 50% of all billionaires in America are Jews?

Based on available evidence, gigantic yields of millions of stolen and destroyed children of defenceless poor people, not feudal agriculture, lured Eastern European Jews to Britain; they changed their names, blended, and latched onto the HUGE STOLEN TRUST FUND.

Latent, but very, very, potent Turf War: Descendants of aliens with camouflage English names oppress, we, the descendants of the robbed with the yields of the robbery.

NEW HEROD: Matthew 2:16: They lie to their simpler children that they are geniuses, and they kill all those who know that they're brainless racist bastards, albeit hands-off.

Dr Richard Dawkins and OECD implied that all the children of Robert Kingston, Director Dobern Property Limited, Solicitor, and Accountant, albeit England's Class, wouldn't be able to read and understand the brainless racist nonsense he immortalised.

"Natural selection will not remove ignorance from future generations." Dr Richard Dawkins.

OYINBO OLE: Ignorant descendants of THIEVES and owners of stolen children of defenceless poor people, including the African ancestors of Meghan Markle's white children - Habakkuk.

Then, they used guns to steal for the benefit of their own people, now, they use racist lies to steal for the benefit of white imbeciles (predominantly but not exclusively white adults with the basic skills of a child) — Habakkuk.

They're scared.

The public must not know that intellect is absolutely unrelated to the indisputably superior skin colour that they neither made not chose.

OECD REPORT:

England's young people are near the bottom of the global league table for basic skills. OECD finds 16- to 24-year-olds have literacy and numeracy levels no better than those of their grandparents' generation.

England is the only country in the developed world where the generation approaching retirement is more literate and numerate than the youngest adults, according to the first skills survey by the Organisation for Economic Co-operation and Development.

In a stark assessment of the success and failure of the 720-million-strong adult workforce across the wealthier economies, the economic think tank warns that in England, adults aged 55 to 65 perform better than 16- to 24-year-olds at foundation levels of literacy and numeracy. The survey did not include people from Scotland or Wales.

The OECD study also finds that a quarter of adults in England have the maths skills of a 10-year-old. About 8.5 million adults, 24.1% of the population, have such basic levels of numeracy that they can manage only one-step tasks in arithmetic, sorting numbers or reading graphs. This is worse than the average in the developed world, where an average of 19% of people were found to have a similarly poor skill base.

AN IMBECILE: AN ADULT WITH THE BASIC SKILLS OF A CHILD.

Facts are sacred.

Unlike Putin's Russia, there are no oil wells or gas fields in Ilford and Jerusalem.

Putin does not want President Zelensky (a Jew) and Ukrainians to be part of our very, very, highly civilised and super-enlightened Free World where white people, only white people, are allowed to tell incompetent racist lies on record, and where an incontrovertible scatter-head, dyslexic, mendacious, and crooked white man, Robert Kingston, could become the Director of Dobern Property Limited, a Solicitor, and an Accountant, albeit England's class, so he used guns to steal Crimea.

The Irish Catholic ancestors of President Joe Biden did not evolve in America. Then, European Christians used guns to dispossess Native Americans, and they stole their land.

"All have taken what had other owners, and all have had recourse to arms rather than quit the prey onto which they were fastened." Dr Samuel Johnson

Ignorant racist bastards.

Ultra-righteous descendants of THIEVES: Extremely nasty and merciless racist murderers, armed robbers, armed land grabbers, industrial-scale professional thieves, gun runners, drug dealers (opium merchants), and owners of stolen poor black children of defenceless Africans, including the Africans ancestors of Meghan Markle's white children — Habakkuk.

Our own NIGERIA, shell's docile cash cow since 1956.

Our own Nigerian babies with huge oil wells and gas fields near their huts, eat only 1.5/day in our own NIGERIA, a

very, very, bellyful, scatter — head, hereditary dyslexic, and
incompetently dishonest white man, whose white mother and
father have never seen crude oil, and whose white ancestors,
including Prime Minister Benjamin Disraeli (1804–1881),
and white ancestors of Winston Churchill (1874–1965), were
fed like battery hens with yields of stolen poor black children
of defenceless Africans, including the African ancestors of
Meghan Markle's white children — Habakkuk, is our
Director Dobern Property Limited, Solicitor, and
Accountant, albeit England's Class — Habakkuk.

Before Slavery, what?

Then, there was only subsistence feudal agriculture.

"Agriculture not only gives riches to a nation, but the only
one she can call her own." Dr Samuel Johnson (1709–1784).

It is plainly deductible that gigantic yields of millions of
stolen poor black children of defenceless Africans, including
the African ancestors of Meghan Markle's white children,
not feudal agriculture, lured the Jewish ancestors of
Benjamin Disraeli (1804–1881) to Great Britain.

If all the Rabbis, in UK, USA, Canada, and Europe,
including Ukraine and Russia, could disprove the truth,
which is that Robert Kingston, Director Dobern Property
Limited, Solicitor, and Accountant, albeit England's Class,

unrelentingly LIED on record, they will confirm the belief of
billions of people in our world, which is that Antichrist
Freemasonry Quasi-Religion (Mediocre Mafia, New
Pharisees, New Good Samaritans, Defenders of Faiths,
including all the faiths and religions — associated with the
15 Holy Books in the House of Commons, and Dissenters of
the faith — John 14:6), Antichrist Islam, Antichrist Judaism,
and all other motley assemblies of exotic religions and faiths
— under the common umbrella of the Governor of the
Church of England, and the Defender of the FAITH — are
not intellectually flawed Satanic Mumbo Jumbo — John
14:6.

Not all idiots are racists, but all racists are thick idiotic
bastards.

The centuries-old unspoken myth that intellect is related to
the universally acknowledged irrefutably superior skin
colour that the very, very, fortunate wearer neither made
nor chose is the mother of all racist scams.

They hate us, and we know.

Facts are sacred, and they cannot be overstated.

It is the honest belief of the author that Helen Falcon (MBE)
is a THIEF, but only by heritage.

Based on cogent, irrefutable, and available evidence, the
entire foundation of Bristol, including Bristol University,
where Mrs Helen Falcon was a student, was built on bones,

bones of stolen poor black children of defenceless Africans, including the African ancestors of Meghan Markle's white children, and more bones than the millions of skulls at the doorstep of Comrade Pol Pot (1925–1998).

When England, inevitably, pays equitable and just reparation, and settles several centuries of accruing interest, she will instantly become poorer than Niger, and there is no uranium in Freemasons' Kempston — Philippian 1:21; was Phillip a closeted white supremacist 33rd Degree Freemason (Scottish Rite)?

There is a transparently just Judge, and every unbalanced will be balanced — John 5:22, Matthew 25: 31–46, Habakkuk.

Irish Joe, how much money did your Catholic ancestors have in their pockets when they disembarked on stolen land, without luggage or decent shoes?

An ignorant descendant of armed European land grabbers.

"All have taken what had other owners, and all have had recourse to arms rather than quit the prey onto which they were fastened." Dr Samuel Johnson

Bedford, England: District Judge Paul Robert Ayers, > 70, a Mason, and the Senior Vice President of the Association of Her Majesty's District Judges, 3, St Paul's Square, MK

40 1SQ, based on available evidence, Nigerien children
with huge uranium mines near their huts eat only 1.5/day in
Niger, West Africa, a bellyful, overfed closeted hereditary
white supremacist bastard whose white father and mother
do not know where, in Africa, Niger is, or the meaning of
the word 'uranium', and whose mentally gentler children
(OECD) mightn't be able to spell uranium, and whose
white ancestors, including ultra-righteous John Bunyan
(1628 – 1688), were fed like battery hens with yields of
millions of stolen and destroyed poor black children of
defenceless Africans, including the African ancestors of
Meghan Markle's white children - was our District Judge
in Bedford.

Ignorance is bliss: "Those who know the least obey the
best." George Farquhar

Mrs Margaret Thatcher (1925 – 2013): "She probably thinks
Sinai is the plural of sinus." Jonathan Aitken

Based on several decades of very, very, proximate
observations and direct experiences, the white man is
grossly overrated. Then, closeted hereditary white
supremacist descendants of Alphonse Gabriel deceived
their own mentally gentler children (OECD) that they were
Archangel Gabriel - Habakkuk.

JUDICIAL DIVERSITY: ACCELERATING CHANGE:
"The near absence of women and Black, Asian and

minority ethnic judges in the senior judiciary, is no longer tolerable. It undermines the democratic legitimacy of our legal system; it demonstrates a denial of fair and equal opportunities to members of underrepresented groups, and the diversity deficit weakens the quality of justice." Sir Geoffrey Bindman, KC, and Karon Monaghan, KC.

Homogeneity in the administration of their legal system is the impregnable secure mask of merciless racist evil— Habakkuk 1:4.

CHAPTER TWELVE: Dr Ngozi Ekweremadu

BEDFORD, ENGLAND: District Judge Paul Robert Ayers, > 70, a Mason, and the Senior Vice President of the Association of Her Majesty's District Judges, 3, St Paul's Square, MK 40 1SQ, based on available evidence, our own money, NIGERIA (oil/gas), is by far more relevant to the economic survival of your white mother, your white father, your white spouse, and all your white children than NORTHAMPTON. Based on available evidence, it is the absolute truth that the white ancestors of your own white mother and father were THIEVES and owners of stolen poor black children of defenceless Africans, including the African ancestors of the white great grandchildren of Prince Phillip (1921 – 2021).

BEDFORD, ENGLAND: District Judge Paul Robert Ayers, > 70, a Mason, and the Senior Vice President of the Association of Her Majesty's District Judges, 3, St Paul's Square, MK 40 1SQ, based on available evidence, you are a racist descendant of righteous professional white thieves, extremely nasty racist murderers, and insatiably greedy owners of stolen poor black children of defenceless Africans, including the African ancestors of Prince Harry's white children — Habakkuk.

Facts are sacred.

"The truth allows no choice." Dr Samuel Johnson

BEDFORD, ENGLAND: District Judge Paul Robert Ayers, > 70, a Mason, and the Senior Vice President of the Association of Her Majesty's District Judges, 3, St Paul's Square, MK 40 1SQ, based on available evidence, you are worthy only because you are white and England is very rich, or what else?

The affluence that your thoroughly wretched white ancestors, mere agricultural labourers, crossed the English Channels, without luggage or decent shoes, to latch onto, was preceded by SLAVERY.

"Affluence is not a birth right." David Cameron.

BEDFORD, ENGLAND: District Judge Paul Robert Ayers, > 70, a Mason, and the Senior Vice President of the Association of Her Majesty's District Judges, 3, St Paul's Square, MK 40 1SQ, based on available evidence, the affluence you implicitly brag about is not the yield of your Christ granted talent, and it is not the yield of the implied Higher IQs of your own white mother and father, and unlike Putin's Russia, there are no oil wells or gas fields in Freemasons' Kempston and where your own white mother and father were born., and industrial revolution was preceded by Slavery; it paid for it.

BEDFORD, ENGLAND: District Judge Paul Robert Ayers, > 70, a Mason, and the Senior Vice President of the Association of Her Majesty's District Judges, 3, St Paul's Square, MK 40 1SQ, based on available evidence, prior to Slavery, there weren't very many proper houses in Bedford, and there was only subsistence feudal agriculture.

"Agriculture not only gives riches to a nation, but the only one she can call her own." Dr Samuel Johnson.

They spin everybody; they destroy all those they cannot spin — New Herod, Matthew 2: 16.

Then, and only there, for their legal system to work as designed, the white imbeciles they shepherd (predominantly but not exclusively white adults with the basic skills of a child) must believe that they are transparently impartial and have supreme knowledge. They are neither impartial nor have supreme knowledge, so they destroy all those, particularly mere Africans, who know that they are crooked closeted hereditary white supremacist bastards.

BEDFORD, ENGLAND: GDC, Sue Gregory, OBE, unrelentingly lied under oath (on record) — Habakkuk 1:4. A very, very, dishonest white woman. A closeted hereditary white supremacist Officer of the Most Excellent Order of our Empire of Stolen Affluence — Habakkuk.

BEDFORD, ENGLAND: District Judge Paul Robert Ayers, > 70, a Mason, and the Senior Vice President of the Association of Her Majesty's District Judges, 3, St Paul's Square, MK 40 1SQ, which part of Statute or legal precedent granted a crooked racist white bastard, albeit an Officer of the Most Excellent Order of our Empire of Stolen Affluence, the right to tell incompetent racist lies — on record?

OUR OWN NIGERIA: SHELL'S DOCILE CASH COW SINCE 1956.

BEDFORD, ENGLAND: District Judge Paul Robert Ayers, > 70, a Mason, and the Senior Vice President of the Association of Her Majesty's District Judges, 3, St Paul's Square, MK 40 1SQ, based on available evidence, unlike Putin's Russia, there are no oil wells or gas fields in Northampton and where your own white mother and father were born — Habakkuk.

Based on several decades of very, very, proximate observations and direct experiences, whites get very, very, angry when blacks know that they're inferior to whites under their law.

Only white people are allowed to tell lies under oath, in their indiscreetly vindictive Negrophobic charade - Habakkuk 1:4.

Racist White Bastards.

OYINBO OLE: Based on several decades of very, very, proximate observations and direct experiences, they hate us, and we know. They're very sad because only their skin colour is superior to ours, NOTHING else is.

If they could, and legally, they will decapitate us.

They hate us with sadistic racist passion, and we know.

They are New King Herod, a lunatic Jew — Matthew 2:16, Matthew 14.

Then, on stolen plantations, in their stolen New World, kidnapped Africans who disagreed with their owners were mercilessly flogged to death, or they were frog-marched to the woods, at gunpoint, stripped naked, and they were hanged from tall trees, and without hoods.

He is transparently just, so our time will come, and we shall extract a tooth for a tooth.

If they love you, it's the conclusive proof that you can't see them, and if they don't, it's proof that you can.

"The white man is the devil." Elijah Mohammed (1897–1975).

"A complaints such as Mrs Bishop's could trigger an enquiry." Stephen Henderson, LLM, BDS, Head at MDDUS, 1 Pemberton Row, London EC4A 3BG.

"I don't want to talk grammar. I want to talk like a lady." George Bernard Shaw.

A brainless scatter-head crooked white man.

WEST AFRICA: Nigerien babies with huge uranium mines near their huts eat only 1.5/day in our own West Africa, a very, very, bellyful overfed scatter head, crooked, and closeted hereditary white supremacist bastard whose white mother and father mightn't know the meaning of uranium, and whose white children mightn't be able to spell the word 'uranium' — is our head at MDDUS, 1 Pemberton Row, London EC4A 3BG.

An ignorant racist white bastard.

Then, the white ancestors of his white mother and father carried and sold millions of stolen poor children of defenceless Africans, including the West African ancestors of Meghan Markle's white children, now, they steal Africa's natural resources, including Niger's uranium.

OYINBO OLE: Unlike Putin's Russia, there are no oil wells or gas fields in Oxford and where the white mother and father of Stephen Henderson, Head at MDDUS, 1 Pemberton Row, London EC4A 3BG, were born.

President Biden and President Zelensky want Ukrainians to be part of our very, very highly civilised, and super-enlightened free world, where a crooked racist white semi-illiterate, Stephen Henderson, is a Head at MDDUS, 1 Pemberton Row, London EC4A 3BG, but President Putin doesn't, so he converted Mariupol from bricks to rubble.

GDC: Ms Rachael Bishop (Senior NHS Nurse) unrelentingly lied under oath — Habakkuk 1:4. Our very, very, dishonest closeted hereditary white supremacist crooked Senior NHS Nurse of our Empire of Stolen Affluence — Habakkuk 1:4.

Then, and only there, when their people committed racist crimes against our people, their people who oversaw the administration of their law (closeted hereditary white supremacist Freemason Judges) criminally buried RACIAL HATRED.

It is not the truth that racial hatred is a myth, and it is not a conspiracy theory, and it is not extinct, and it is considerably more common than ordinarily realised.

CHAPTER THIRTEEN: Apartheid by stealth. An African whistleblower.

A brainless closeted hereditary white supremacist bastard sat on a highchair that his white daddy and mummy couldn't and didn't buy, in a Magnificent Cathedral Court that was preceded by SLAVERY (future flats).

29, Goldington Road is a block of flats.

An ignorant descendant of THIEVES and owners of stolen poor black children of defenceless Africans, including the NIGERIAN ancestors of Meghan Markle's white children – Habakkuk.

Meghan Markle says she is 43% Nigerian.

"Britons stank." W.S.

William Shakespeare wouldn't know because he was not a lady's man. At least one of Wole Soyinka's wives, and some of his concubines were Britons.

Which one of our putrid tubes did our Born-Again Christian, a Briton, tell our Bedford's Freemason District Judge and Freemasons at Brickhill Baptist Church, Bedford, she used to work for £0.5M, the dorsal stinking tube, or the ventral one?

Our Born-Again Christian pays tithe (quasi-protection money) and prays to Christ at Brickhill Baptist Church, and members of the very, very, charitable Antichrist Freemasonry Quasi-Religion (Mediocre Mafia, New Pharisees, New Good Samaritans, Defenders of Faiths, and the Defender of the Faith — John 14:6) in Kempton, Bedfordshire Masonic Centre, the Keep, Bedford Road, MK42 8AH, seemed to answer all her prayers.

OXFORD, ENGLAND: GDC, British Soldier, albeit only a Territorial Defender, Stephanie Twidale (TD) unrelentingly lied under oath — Habakkuk 1:4.

A very, very, dishonest white woman.

A closeted hereditary white supremacist British Soldier of our Empire of Stolen Affluence.

Facts are sacred, and they cannot be overstated.

In the future, AI will settle disputes among imbeciles (adults with the basic skills of a child), and they will be considerably fairer than incontrovertibly functional semi-illiterate closeted hereditary white supremacist Freemason Judges — Habakkuk 1:4.

Then, and only there, based on very cogent, irrefutable, and available evidence, and very, very, proximate observations and direct experiences, when their people committed racist crimes against our people, their people who oversaw the administration of their law (closeted hereditary white supremacist Freemason Judges), criminally buried RACIAL HATRED.

Based on contacts, Stephanie Twidale (TD), the seemingly dementing or demented white woman (incipient Alzheimer's disease), had a very distinct body odour.

Stephanie Twidale (TD), the closeted hereditary white supremacist Briton, stank.

All Nigerians and Nigeriens, are THIEVES, so closeted hereditary white supremacist bastards, descendants of very, very, highly civilised, super-enlightened, industrial-scale professional thieves, extremely nasty, vicious, and merciless racist murderers, gun runners, drug dealers (opium merchants), and owners of stolen poor black children of defenceless Africans, including the African ancestors of Meghan Markle's white children, resorted to vindictive racist criminality — in pursuant of curing the disease of thievery of African thieves.

CHAPTER FOURTEEN: Dr Ngozi Ekweremadu

Thou shall not steal — was in every Bible, including during European Christians' extortionately profitable commerce in millions of stolen poor black children of defenceless Africans (slavery), including the African ancestors of Meghan Markle's white children – Habakkuk.

Leviticus 19:11–13 New King James Version (NKJV). 'You shall not steal, nor deal falsely, nor lie to one another.

Then, members of the vulgarly very, very, charitable Freemasonry Quasi-Religion (Mediocre Mafia, New Pharisees, New Good Samaritans, Defenders of Faiths, including all exotic Faiths and/or Religions associated with the 15 Holy Books in the House of Commons, and Dissenters of the Faith – John 14:6) wear vulgar Pharisees' charitable works as cloaks of deceit, and they buy very, very, colourful shiny aprons, with vulgar embroideries, and they use them to decorate the temples of their powerless and useless fertility tools, and the closeted hereditary white supremacist bastards lie that they don't lie — Psalm 144.

When Freedom of Expression becomes a universal basic right for all, their intellectually flawed Satanic Mumbo Jumbo will be uncovered and irreversibly destroyed.

Ignorant closeted hereditary white supremacist bastards see molecules, and the conceited, deluded, confused, and very, very, shallow members of the brainlessly and baselessly If-awarded superior race destroy all Nigerians who see quarks.

"The supreme vice is shallowness." Wilde

They are the New Herod, and like the intolerant lunatic Jew, they brainlessly and baselessly awarded themselves the supreme knowledge, and they vindictively destroy all their enemies and/or all those who disagree with them - Matthew 2:16, Matthew 14.

If all the 33rd Degree White Freemason Judges in Great Britain (Scottish Rite), predominantly but not exclusively white, could disprove the truth that Bedford's District Judge was an impostor, an expert of distortion, and a functional semi-illiterate, and disprove the truth that Bedford's District Judge unrelentingly lied or otherwise deviated from the truth, under oath (approved Judgement), and if they could disprove the truth that OXFORD, ENGLAND: GDC, British Soldier, albeit only a Territorial Defender, Stephanie Twidale (TD) unrelentingly lied under oath — Habakkuk 1:4, they will confirm the belief of scores of millions of Britons, which is that very, very, charitable Antichrist Freemasonry Quasi-Religion (Mediocre Mafia, New Pharisees, New Good Samaritans, Defenders of Faiths, and Dissenters of the Faith — John 14:6), Antichrist Islam, Antichrist Judaism, and all other motley assemblies of Faiths and Religions, under the common umbrella of the HM, the Governor of the Church of

England, and the Defender of the Faith (John 14:6), are not intellectually flawed Satanic Mumbo Jumbo, and they will also confirm that reasoning and vision have boundaries, and if reasoning and vision have boundaries, He lied when He disclosed pictures His purportedly unbounded mind painted, and He lied when He audaciously stated that He was exceptional — John 14:6. If the fellow told the truth, before Romans, and Jews, in the Council, we are all FORKED, as His Knights attack Kings and Queens simultaneously, and only Queens can move — Checkmate.

"It does no harm to throw the occasional man overboard, but it does not do much good if you are steering full speed ahead for the rocks." Sir Ian Gilmour (1926 – 2007)

Facts are sacred, and they cannot be overstated.

CHAPTER FIFTEEN: Apartheid by stealth. An African whistleblower.

NIGEL FARAGE: "We are living in an increasingly lawless society. Thieves and shoplifters must be convicted!"

An ignorant descendant of THIEVES.

A closeted hereditary white supremacist descendant of THIEVES and owners of stolen children of defenceless Africans, including the African ancestors of Meghan Markle's white children — Habakkuk.

NIGEL FARAGE: The white ancestors of your white mother and father were THIEVES too, and they were owners of stolen poor black children of defenceless Africans, including the African ancestors of Meghan Markle's white children.

The greedy, racist, and crooked white bastard thieves, your white ancestors) cannot be convicted only because they are no longer here, but the inheritors of their gigantic loot remain here, and they should pay reparation to balance the unbalanced.

Then, they carried and sold millions of stolen children of defenceless Africans, including the African ancestors of Meghan Markle's white children, now, they steal natural resources from AFRICA, including Nigerians' oil and gas, and Nigeriens' uranium.

"Trump's administration packed Courts with white Judges."
Kamala Harris.

Did Kamala Harris imply that Trump's administration packed courts with mediocre white Freemason Judges (Mediocre Mafia, New Pharisees, New Good Samaritans, Defenders of Motley Assemblies of Exotic Faiths, and Dissenters of the Faith — John 14:6)?

Then, all Judges were white, and most of them were white supremacist Freemasons (occultist and quasi-voodoo-men), and some of them were thicker than a tonne of planks.

Bedford, England: District Judge Paul Robert Ayers, > 70, a Mason, and the Senior Vice President of the Association of Her Majesty's District Judges, of 3, St Paul's Square, MK 40 1SQ, which part of Bedfordshire Masonic Centre (Territorial Defence), the Keep, Bedford Road, Kempston, MK42 8AH, was not stolen, or which part of it is the yield of the Higher IQs of your own white mother and father, or which part of it preceded SLAVERY: The building or its chattels?

The USA is the real territorial defender of Europe, and absolutely everything else is an auxiliary bluff.

Very, very, charitable closeted white supremacist Masons, occultist defenders of motley assemblies of exotic faiths, and dissenters of the faith – John 14:6, seem to believe that they are intellectually superior to all NIGERIANS, if they are, the closeted racist white bastards, deluded Antichrist racist thugs, half-educated school drop-outs and their superiors who have informal access to some very, very, powerful closeted white supremacist Freemason Judges, should play with straight bats, and objectively prove their brainlessly and baselessly assumed intellectual superiority.

"Ethical Foreign Policy." Robin Cook (1946–2005).

There are Freemasons in Ukraine.

Occultist quasi-voodoo men (Freemasons): Their people are everywhere, and they control almost everything.

Bedfordshire Masonic Centre, the Keep (Territorial Defence), Bedford Road, Kempston, MK42 8AH: Integrity, Friendship, Respect, and Charity.

The Grand Masonic Temple, the Mother Lodge, 60 Great Queen St, London WC2B 5AZ. If Freemasons, Occultist Defenders of Faiths, and Dissenters of the Faith — John 14:6, are as ethical and as brave as they seem to imply, why didn't the closeted white supremacist bastards foresee that

Putin will convert Mariupol from bricks to rubble, and why did they look away while he did?

In 1892, armed racist white bastards, and those they armed, used heavy guns to mercilessly slaughter almost everyone in our tribe, in the African bush – IJEBU.

Google: Imagbon 1892.

Those who need a fairer fight should, directly, use guns to evict Putin from Crimea, he stole it with guns.

A brainless racist white bastard. An ignorant descendant of undocumented refugees, mere agricultural labourers (peasants), from Eastern Europe, with arbitrarily acquired camouflage English names.

The racist white bastard gave the game away when he approved and immortalised what his semi-literate white mother and father spoke, which his poly-educated white supervisors in Luton authorised.

CHAPTER SIXTEEN: Dr Ngozi Ekweremadu

HHJ Perusko studied law at polytechnic: Not Russell Group Inferior Education — Proverbs 17:16.

John 14:6: Bedford, England, District Judge Paul Robert Ayers, > 70, a Mason, and the Senior Vice President of the Association of Her Majesty's District Judges, of 3, St Paul's Square, MK 40 1SQ, reasoning and vision have no finite boundaries, and the fellow told the truth when He disclosed pictures His unbounded mind painted, it is possible to use cogent facts and irrefutable evidence to irreversibly destroy you and the indiscreetly institutionally racist legal system that you serve. Based on cogent and irrefutable evidence, our own money, NIGERIA (oil/gas), is by far more relevant to the economic survival of all your own white children, your white spouse, your white father, and your white mother than Northampton. Unlike Putin's Russia, there are no oil wells or gas fields in Freemasons' Kempston. Based on available evidence, the white ancestors of your white mother and father were THIEVES and owners of stolen poor black children of defenceless Africans, including the African ancestors of Prince Harry's white children - Habakkuk.

Facts are sacred, and they cannot be overstated.

White Supremacy is the bedrock of White Privilege. Then, it was the brainless and baseless birth right of members of the self-awarded superior race to be intellectually superior to all Nigerians, and since they weren't, closeted white supremacist bastards resorted to racist Judicial terrorism, and they stole yields of our Christ granted talents.

"England will fight to the last American." American saying.

Their hairs stand on end when they are challenged by NIGERIANS, we and our type are the ones closeted white supremacist bastards will beat up without the support of the YANKS.

Very, very, highly civilised, and super-enlightened white Christians' proxy war over Africa's huge and varied natural resources: The most diverse solid minerals reserve in the world.

Why is it that very, very, highly civilised industrialised Christian Countries set up shops (Military Bases) only in African Countries with natural resources and raw materials they need? A case in point, then, France carried and sold thousands of stolen children from West Africa, including Niger, now, they steal natural resources, including uranium from Niger.

After several continuous centuries of barbarous, crude, cruel, and sadistic European Christians' commerce in millions of stolen children of defenceless Africans, the succeeding partition of Africa (1884) was basically caused by their desire for raw materials, natural resources, and marketing.

Then, very, very, highly civilised greedy racist bastards carried and sold millions of stolen children of poor people (Africans), including the African ancestors of Meghan Markle's white children, now, they steal natural resources from our own Africa - Habakkuk.

Bedford, England: District Judge Paul Robert Ayers, > 70, a Mason, and the Senior Vice President of the Association of Her Majesty District Judges, which part of our County Court, 3, St Paul's Square, MK 40 1SQ, was not stolen, or which part of it is the yield of your talent, or which part of it is the yield of the Higher IQs of your own white mother and father, or which part of it did transparent virtue yield, or which part of it did the good people of Bedford buy, or which part of it preceded SLAVERY: The building or its chattels?

Ignorance is bliss.

Very, very, hardened racist descendants of undocumented refugees from Eastern Europe oppress African descendants of the robbed with yields of the robbery: Latent but very, very, potent Turf War. A brainless racist white bastard: He is incontrovertibly a functional semi-illiterate, the land on which his white mother and father were born is natural resources poor, and yields only food, unlike Putin's Russia, there are no oil wells or gas fields where his own white mother and father were born, he is relatively rich, and he dishonestly implied that he did not know that the white ancestors of his white mother and father were extremely nasty racist murders, industrial-scale professional thieves, and owners of stolen children of defenceless poor people (Africans), including the African ancestors of the niece and nephew of the Prince of Wales.

CHAPTER SEVENTEEN: Apartheid by stealth. An African Whistleblower

"**M**any Scots masters were considered among the most brutal, with life expectancy on their plantations averaging a mere four years. We worked them to death then simply imported more to keep the sugar and thus the money flowing. Unlike centuries of grief and murder, an apology cost nothing. So, what does Scotland have to say?" Herald Scotland: Ian Bell, Columnist, Sunday 28 April 2013.

BEDFORD, ENGLAND: District Judge Paul Robert Ayers, > 70, a Mason, and the Senior Vice President of the Association of Her Majesty District Judges, 3, St Paul's Square, MK 40 1SQ, why is England very, very, rich?

Is affluence the yield of the supposedly Higher IQs of your own white mother and father, or is it the yield of your extraordinary talent, or what?

Unlike Putin's Russia, there are no oil wells or gas fields In Northampton and where your own white mother and father were born.

Based on available evidence, the white ancestors of your white mother and father were THIEVES and owners of stolen poor black children of defenceless Africans, including the African ancestors of Meghan Markle's white children.

Their law is equal for blacks and whites, but its administration is not, and when their people commit racist crimes against Africans, their people who oversee the administration of their law criminally bury racial hatred—Habakkuk.

They are not the only creation of Almighty God, and the universally acknowledged irrefutably superior skin colour is not the only wonder of our world.

Probably as recommended by Freemasons at Brickhill Baptist Church, Bedford, for several years, and unbeknownst to the child's father, the psychotic Born-Again Christian (Hypothyroidism psychosis complicated by religious psychosis), regularly drove the unfortunate child to Bedfordshire Masonic Centre, the Keep, Bedford Road, Kempston, MK42 8AH, for extra-lessons to supplement the stereotypically Negro learning Disability Education that was imposed on the Nigerian child without the knowledge or comment of his father.

They want to help us, armed racist bastards who carried and sold millions of stolen poor black children of defenceless Africans, including the African ancestors of Prince Harry's white children, did not come to Africa to help African children, they came to Africa purely for economic gain—to carry and sell millions of stolen poor black children of defenceless Africans. If members of the very, very, charitable Freemasonry Quasi-Religion are as clever as they seem to imply, why are the sheep they shepherd among the least literate and the least numerate in the industrialised world (OECD).

When it became apparent to them that Christ was intellectually unplayable, they killed Him, and solely to prevent Him from speaking. Then, black people (Africans) were inferior under their law, and very, very, highly civilised white European Christians became very, very, angry when self-educated Africans refused to become actors and pretend that they were equal to members of the brainlessly and baselessly self-awarded superior race under their law, and always before closeted white supremacist Freemason Judges.

OXFORD, ENGLAND: Based on available evidence, GDC, Helen Falcon (MBE), Member of the Most Excellent Order of our Empire unrelentingly lied under oath (on record) — Habakkuk 1:4. A Closeted Racist Crooked Member of the Most Excellent Order of Empire. "Affluence is not a birth right." David Cameron. Like our universe, our Empire did not evolve from NOTHING, then, almost everything was actively and deliberately stolen with guns. The only black closeted white supremacist bastards truly love is our money (Africa's natural resources and raw materials). Then, greedy racist bastards carried and sold millions of stolen children of defenceless Africans, now, they steal natural resources from Africa.

BEDFORD, ENGLAND: GDC, Sue Gregory (OBE)unrelentingly lied under oath(on record). A Racist

Officer of the Most Excellent Order of our Empire of Stolen Affluence — Habakkuk.

Then, the job of closeted white supremacist Freemason Judges was to legally justify hereditary racial hatred.

There will be more equality and fairness in the administration of English Law when the probability of the Judge being white is not 100%.

Homogeneity in the administration of English Law is the impregnable secure mask of merciless racist evil.

"All sections of UK society are institutionally racist." Sir Bernard Hogan—Howe, a former Metropolitan Police Chief.

Closeted White Supremacist Freemason Judges are human beings: Some human beings are RACISTS.

The Judiciary, the Police Force, and the very, very, Charitable Freemasonry Fraternity are sections of UK society.

Is stealing hereditary?

If there is irrefutable evidence that the white ancestors of one's white mother and father were industrial-scale professional thieves and owners of stolen poor children of defenceless Africans, including the African ancestors of Prince Harry's white children, it will be very naive not to expect racial hatred complicated by incompetent mendacity to be part of one's genetic inheritances.

Then, everyone was white. If we are not very, very, smart, why are we very, very, rich? Shepherds did not bring stolen African children home, they carried and sold them elsewhere, and they lied to their own mentally gentler white children that they were paragons of wisdom and virtue who, like Mother Teresa of Calcutta, did only virtuous works in Africa.

Their irreparably corrupt legal system that is overseen by closeted white supremacist Freemason Judges, essentially, for the benefit of white people – Habakkuk 1:4.

Closeted white supremacist Freemason Judges know how to steal for white people, but ultra-righteous racist white bastards don't know how to repair the scatter-heads of white people.

Bedford's District Judge Paul Robert Ayers, > 70, a Mason, and the Senior Vice President of the Association of Her Majesty's District Judges, of 3, St Paul's Square, MK 40 1SQ, our own money, Nigeria (oil/gas) is by far more relevant to the economic survival of all your own white children, your white spouse, your white father, and your white mother than Northampton. Unlike Putin's Russia, there are no oil wells or gas fields in Freemasons' Kempston and where your own white mother and father were born. If there is irrefutable evidence that the white ancestors of one's white mother and father were THIEVES and owners of stolen poor children of defenceless Africans, including the African ancestors of Kamala Harris, it is plainly deductible that Freedom of Expression is not one's friend.

"Meghan Markle was the victim of explicit and obnoxious racial hatred." John Bercow (a former speaker).

Had she been a proper Negro, she would have been butchered like Stephen Lawrence (1974–1993).

She is 57% Caucasian, and only 43% Nigerian.

Bedford, England: Freemason, Brother, Richard William Hill (NHS — Postgraduate Tutor) fabricated reports and unrelentingly lied under oath.

A racist white man. An ignorant descendant of ultra-righteous WHITE THIEVES and owners of stolen poor black children of defenceless Africans — Habakkuk.

A very, very, dishonest white man. A closeted racist crooked white Freemason.

Facts are sacred, and they cannot be overstated.

Charitable Freemasons: Closeted white supremacist bastards, and defenders of motley assemblies of exotic faiths, they tell incompetent racist lies under oath (on record), and they tell lies all the time.

"Lies are told all the time." Sir Michael Havers (1923 – 1992).

Closeted white supremacist dissenters of the faith — John 14:6 constructively invited Nigerian Dissenters of Faiths to deny that the fellow is who He says He is.

If all the white Freemason Judges in Great Britain (predominantly but not exclusively white) could disprove the truth that their own kindred, Freemason, Brother, Richard William Hill (NHS — Postgraduate Tutor) fabricated reports and unrelentingly lied under oath, they will, concomitantly, confirm the belief of all the white Freemason Judges in Great Britain (predominantly but not exclusively white), which is that the fellow is not exceptional, and John 14:6, the faith, is intellectually flawed.

If they were as smart as they implied, why didn't they foresee that the Corporal would flip, and why didn't they help themselves when he did.

Then, greedy bastards won in courts, but in the war, when
the Corporal flipped, the only transparently true Judge
looked away—John 5:22, Matthew 25: 31–46, and very,
very, greedy bastards lost everything, and more.

Jews are not our God.

How come only 1.4% of Americans are Jews, but 50% of
billionaires in America are Jews?

"Jews are intelligent and creative, Chinese are intelligent but
not create, Indians are servile, and Africans are morons."
Professor James Dewey Watson (DNA) paraphrased.

Judas Iscariot, Ghislaine Maxwell's dad, Ján Ludvík Hyman
Binyamin Hoch, and Bernard Madoff were Jews.

Gigantic yields of millions of stolen poor children of
defenceless Africans, including the African ancestors of
Meghan Markle's white children, not feudal agriculture,
lured Eastern European Jews to Great Britain.

"It was our arms in the river of Cameroon, put into the hands
of the trader, that furnished him with the means of pushing
his trade; and I have no more doubt that they are British
arms, put into the hands of Africans, which promote
universal war and desolation that I can doubt their having
done so in that individual instance. I have shown how great is
the enormity of this evil, even on the supposition that we take

only convicts and prisoners of war. But take the subject in
another way, and how does it stand? Think of 80,000 persons
carried out of their native country by we know not what
means! For crimes imputed! For light or inconsiderable
faults! For debts perhaps! For crime of witchcraft! Or a
thousand other weak or scandalous pretexts! Reflect on
80,000 persons annually taken off! There is something in the
horror of it that surpasses all bounds of imagination." —
Prime Minister William Pitt the Younger.

Deceptively schooled ultra-righteousness and vulgar
Pharisees' charitable works without equitable reparation, and
the settlement of several centuries of accruing unpaid interest
— are continuing racist fraud.

ABOUT THE AUTHOR.

The author, like the ancestors of Meghan Markle, was born
in Nigeria, and for several years, he was a boarder at the
University of Lagos.

Printed in Great Britain
by Amazon

27518846R00106